BOOKCASES, CABINETS & BUILT-INS

The Taunton Press

Inspiration for hands-on living®

THE TAUNTON PRESS, INC.
63 South Main Street
Newtown, CT 06470-2344
e-mail: tp@taunton.com

EDITOR: Jennifer Renjilian Morris
COPY EDITOR: Marc Sichel
INDEXER: Jay Kreider
COVER: Teresa Fernandes
INTERIOR DESIGN: Carol Singer
LAYOUT: Susan Lampe-Wilson

Fine Homebuilding® is a trademark of The Taunton Press, Inc., registered in the U.S. Patent and Trademark Office.

Fine Woodworking® is a trademark of The Taunton Press, Inc., registered in the U.S. Patent and Trademark Office.

The following names/manufacturers appearing in *Bookcases, Cabinets & Built-Ins,* are trademarks: Accuride®; Amana Tool®; Blum® Tandem®; Deft®; Europly®; Fastcap®; Festool® Domino®; Freud®; Google® SketchUp®; Grass®; Hardwoods-Woodworks, Inc.®; Kreg®; Masonite®; Minwax®; Rockler Woodworking and Hardware℠; Sub-Zero®; Waterlox®; White River Woodcraft®; Zinsser® SealCoat®; ZipWall®

Library of Congress Cataloging-in-Publication Data
Bookcases, cabinets & built-ins / editors of Fine homebuilding and Fine woodworking.
    p. cm.
  Includes index.
  ISBN 978-1-60085-758-4
1. Bookcases. 2. Cabinetwork. 3. Built-in furniture. I. Taunton Press. II. Fine homebuilding. III. Fine woodworking. IV. Title: Bookcases, cabinets and built-ins.
  TT197.B595 2012
  684.1'62--dc23

                    2012022205

Printed in the United States of America
20 19 18 17 16 15 14 13

ABOUT YOUR SAFETY: Working wood is inherently dangerous. Using hand or power tools improperly or ignoring safety practices can lead to permanent injury or even death. Don't try to perform operations you learn about here (or elsewhere) unless you're certain they are safe for you. If something about an operation doesn't feel right, don't do it. Look for another way. We want you to enjoy the craft, so please keep safety foremost in your mind whenever you're in the shop.

ACKNOWLEDGMENTS

Special thanks to the authors, editors, art directors, copy editors, and other staff members of *Fine Homebuilding* and *Fine Woodworking* who contributed to the development of the articles in this book.

Contents

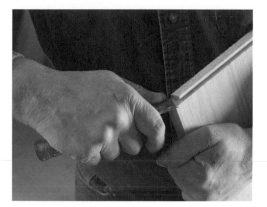

Introduction

What do you see when you look at a sheet of plywood? If you have never built a bookcase, a cabinet, or a built-in, you may see only a rectangular sheet of material with two curiously different surfaces that seems quite awkward to lug around. On the other hand, if you already understand the basics of building bookcases, cabinets, and built-ins, then you probably see boundless possibilities: a Craftsman-style hutch; a Shaker-style pantry; a modern, frameless kitchen.

Therein lies the beauty of these projects. The basic construction—a solid wood face frame applied to a square plywood case—is often the same for a small, painted bookcase as it is for a full, stain-grade library. Now, that's not to say you should rush out and try to tackle a kitchen's worth of cabinetry as a first project, but I can say from my own experience that the learning curve for these projects is rather gentle. So you can quickly hone your skills with some simple shelves or a bathroom vanity first, and then move on to, say, an entertainment center or a custom kitchen cabinet. If you have bookcases, built-ins, or cabinets to build, this book is for you.

Taken from the pages of *Fine Homebuilding* and *Fine Woodworking* magazines, the articles in this book are written by professionals who mastered the basics long ago and are now ready to share what they have learned with you. If you are just starting out and are confused by the various types of plywood available, we've got you covered. If you are a pro who could use some ideas to speed up production, we've got you covered. And if you need some design inspiration or clever storage ideas, we've got you covered there too—which brings me to the other reason bookcases, cabinets, and built-ins are so cool: Not only are they fun to build, but done well, they also add style, function, and value to your home.

Build well.

—Brian Pontolilo
Editor, *Fine Homebuilding*

Build Better Cabinets with the Best Plywood

MATTHEW TEAGUE

Choosing the right plywood for your next cabinet entails more than just picking the species you want and backing your truck up to the loading dock. You want to make sure you're spending money where it counts: on structurally sound cores where it matters and on fine veneers where they're visible.

Core options

Plywood is commonly available in four different core combinations. Each has unique features that can affect the strength and look of cabinets whether they are stain grade or paint grade.

Veneer core: Superior strength, at a price

This plywood has multiple layers of thin (usually ½ in. and thinner) solid wood that's glued up in a cross-grain orientation. Typical ¾-in. plywood is made of five ½-in. core layers and two face veneers. Although this is the strongest of all core options, imperfections in the core veneers can telegraph through to the face veneers, leaving surfaces that are not perfectly smooth. That said, superior strength, screw retention, and light weight make it appealing to work with.

Veneer core

MDF core: Best choice for a smooth finish

This plywood has a solid piece of medium density fiberboard (MDF) in place of the five core layers in veneer-core plywood. Weight and dust are two downsides, but MDF creates a dead-flat panel that doesn't have any telegraphing issues. Screw retention is good, though it's best to drill pilot holes and to use fasteners designed for engineered wood, like Confirmat screws. The edges of MDF-core plywood can be profiled and finished, unlike other plywood that must be edge-banded in most applications.

MDF core

Particleboard core: Cheap, but difficult to work

Particleboard-core plywood is similar to MDF-core plywood in both construction and characteristics. The panels are flat, retain fasteners well (with the same caveats as MDF), and are among the least expensive plywood sheets available. However, particleboard-core plywood is the most susceptible to tearout when cutting, routing, or drilling.

Combination core: Strong core, smooth face

Combination-core plywood consists of a traditional veneer core, except that the outer layers of the core are made of MDF. Combi-core, as it's often called, offers (almost) the

Particleboard core

Putting It All Together

INTERIOR SURFACES
To save hours of work finishing the inside of cabinets, opt for a prefinished interior surface. Plywood is available as prefinished 1-side or 2-side stock. For a painted exterior, use prefinished 1-side. Prefinished random-match or rotary-cut maple and birch are usually available at the same prices as unfinished plywood.

DRAWER BOXES
Drawer boxes are typically built with Baltic birch or ApplePly (photo below). They are similar products glued up with more layers of wood (18 mm, comparable to ¾-in. plywood, is made of 13 layers, for instance) and generally have fewer surface imperfections. Not all grades are clear, however, so it's worth knowing what you're buying. Baltic birch is sold in grades B, BB, CP, and C, with more imperfections as you progress down the list. Most of what is used for drawer parts is midgrades sold as "shop birch." Choose higher grades, or spend less on lower grades and work around the imperfections.

Combination
core

CABINET BACKS
Use ½-in. prefinished veneer-core plywood in the back of the cabinet for strength and rigidity. Rotary-cut veneer or random-match veneer is perfectly adequate here.

best of both worlds: the smooth, flat faces characteristic of MDF and the strength attributes of veneer core. It's also only slightly heavier than veneer core.

So which core option is best for me?

There's little dispute that an MDF core produces the smoothest, flattest surface, making it the best choice where finishing is concerned. Keep in mind that painted plywood is subject to the same considerations as clear-finished or stained plywood. Paint can actually be worse at highlighting irregularities in the plywood face. If you're looking for an easier material to work with, choose combi-core plywood, which offers nearly the same performance attributes.

Veneer options

Plywood veneers are either rotary-cut or sliced. Rotary-cut veneers are produced from the log in the same way you pull tape from a roll. The cut produces a wild, variegated grain pattern that is cost-effective but generally less attractive. Sliced veneer is cut from the log in much the same way a log is cut into lumber, so it yields veneer that mimics solid stock rather well.

CABINET ENDS
Plank-matched veneer dresses up an exposed face. A plank match mimics the look of edge-glued boards of various widths. It has a less refined look, but is arguably more authentic looking.

Rotary-cut veneer

Rotary-cut veneer: Suitable for painted surfaces and hidden parts

Rotary-cut veneer is a perfectly adequate and economical veneer for use on hidden parts of a cabinet, like the back and the drawers. For the exterior and interior faces of painted work, a rotary-cut veneer with a B or better grade is sufficient. Opt for either birch or maple. (See the sidebar below for an explanation of veneer grading.)

Sliced veneer: Best for stained or clear-finished components

Of all the ways that sliced veneers can be oriented, you'll most commonly find bookmatched and random-matched orientations. Bookmatching looks the best in most applications. It has alternating sheets of veneer from a single flitch opened like a book to create a mirrored-grain pattern. Common on back faces, random-match veneers cost the least, but vary in width, color, and grain. Plank-matched veneer (see drawing, p. 7) is a good option on exposed faces. It's usually a special order and is laid up in a deliberately mismatched pattern to look more natural.

Bookmatching. This A-grade cherry veneer is bookmatched, so the grain patterns mirror each other across the panel. It's among the most attractive orientations, particularly for stain-grade cabinets.

Which veneer option is best for me?

For cabinets receiving a clear or stained finish, use a B or better face veneer. For the back veneer, select a 1 or 2 grade, depending on the project. Book-matched faces look best when the splice is centered on a panel, even if it results in added waste. If a panel is so wide that it includes a second splice line, the mirrored effect becomes lost or muddled. In these cases, a plank match would be a good option. For the inside of the cabinet, a rotary-cut or random-match veneer is perfectly suitable.

Veneer grading

Veneers from a log are segregated into six face grades (AA, A, B, C, D, E) and four back grades (1, 2, 3, 4), with back grades being aesthetically inferior. The best face and back veneers are clear, while successive grades have more noticeable knots, mineral streaks, and color variation.

Plank-matched cherry, face-grade A.

Plank-matched cherry, face-grade B.

Plank-matched cherry, face-grade C.

Illustrated Guide to Drawers

MATTHEW TEAGUE

Whether it's a tiny drawer in a jewelry box or the wide, deep drawer of a dresser, all drawers are little more than a box that slides into an opening. But there are nearly endless combinations of construction methods that can be used to build that box. By understanding the various ways in which drawers are made, you'll be able to choose the best construction method for your project, with the ideal blend of beauty, strength, and efficiency.

Drawers can be made of solid wood, plywood, or both. Drawer fronts often become the focal points of a piece, showing off spectacular figure, molded edges, or a handsome pull. The actual drawer front can be integral to the drawer (see p. 11), meaning that it is joined directly to the drawer sides, or it can be attached to a fully constructed drawer box (called a false front; see p. 12). Joinery options at both the back and front can range from simple butt joints to classic hand-cut dovetails. Drawer bottoms can be made from solid wood or plywood.

To size a drawer correctly, you need to know not only the size of the opening, but also the depth of the inset. Drawers can be designed flush to, recessed into, or overlapping the front of the case.

Different styles of furniture call for different types of drawers. While a plywood drawer with a false front makes sense in a shop cabinet, it would be quite out of place in

Options abound—from simple to refined.
There are a number of great ways to build a drawer. A utility or light-duty drawer might be a simple plywood box with a false front (top) and a plywood bottom. A pinned rabbet offers a simple yet stylish way to build a drawer with an integral front (second from top). Another step up is a drawer made with sliding dovetails and a solid-wood bottom (third from top). The holy grail of drawers (bottom) has hand-cut half-blind dovetails at the front, through-dovetails at the back, and an elegant raised-panel, solid-wood bottom.

a high-style 18th-century reproduction. The joinery and materials you choose should fit the type of furniture you want to build. So should the way the drawer will slide in and out of its pocket. So let's start there.

Drawer slides influence design and construction

Like all drawer decisions, drawer-slide options range from simple and efficient to finely handcrafted. Traditionally, the sides of a wooden drawer slide directly on a wooden frame within the case. Most drawers with integral fronts work well with this design because the drawer is sized and constructed to fit the opening.

Manufactured drawer slides have long been common on kitchen cabinets, but they're being used more and more on high-end furniture today. Although frowned upon by some purists, contemporary slide designs install quickly and painlessly, and it's difficult to find fault with their smooth action, soft-close mechanisms, and full-extension capability. These slides can be side- or bottom-mounted, and are perfect for use with false-front drawers or drawers with sliding dovetails.

Each type of commercial slide has its own drawer requirements, so you'll have to build the drawer to accommodate the slides. For instance, side-mounted slides typically require ½ in. of space on both sides of the drawer box. If you're using commercial slides, it's a good idea to have them on hand before you build either the case or the drawers.

Front joints are the critical ones

Regardless of whether a drawer has an integral front or a false front, most pulling and racking stresses on a drawer box occur at the front corners; after all, a drawer is

Traditional drawer construction uses integral fronts so the drawer is one piece.

opened and closed by pulling and pushing on the front. Any action that isn't straight in or out of the drawer pocket also causes racking stress, which hits the front-corner joints hardest.

For these reasons, front-corner joints should be as strong as possible and have some mechanical reinforcement. This mechanical connection can be as simple as pegs or pins in a rabbet joint, or it can be the interlocking strength of the classic half-blind dovetail.

Integral-front drawers

A traditional drawer is built with the front joined directly to the sides. This is the most lightweight and attractive design overall. Aim for drawer sides that are half to one-third the thickness of the front. Once the drawer has been assembled, the sides often must be planed or sanded carefully so the drawer fits in the opening. In most cases, the joinery is hidden from the front for a clean look.

Rabbet Joints The pinned rabbet is easy to make, but it's not very strong. It should be reinforced with some kind of fastener, such as recessed screws, cut copper nails, or wooden dowels or pegs, which offer a clean, handmade look. With this style of construction, the back of the drawer is usually set into simple dadoes in the drawer sides.

Although it takes a few more tool setups, a half-blind tongue and rabbet adds built-in mechanical strength (beyond glue alone) to the joint. Dado or dadoed rabbet joints are suitable options for the back of the drawer.

A dovetailed rabbet is stronger and more attractive than a simple rabbet joint. This type of corner joint also should be reinforced with pegs, brads, or some kind of mechanical fastener. The rear joints can be rabbeted dadoes (see the drawing at bottom right) or sliding dovetail joints.

Box joints The box joint is the beefier, more handsome cousin of the finger joint (see the bottom left drawing on p. 14), and it's quite comfortable at the front of a piece of furniture. The design seen in the drawing below, reminiscent of Greene-and-Greene construction, features wide fingers with rounded corners. Square, pillowed pegs reinforce the joint and add visual interest. If you're using box joints at the front of a drawer, it's efficient to use them at the back, too, though the fingers should not protrude.

Rabbet Joints

Rabbet should be half to two-thirds as thick as the drawer front.

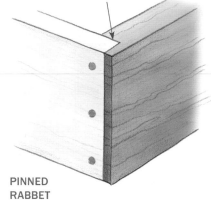

PINNED RABBET

Tongue adds mechanical strength to resist pulling forces.

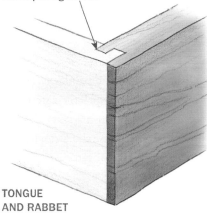

TONGUE AND RABBET

Box Joint

Joint can be reinforced with pegs at the top and bottom, or through the front or sides (shown).

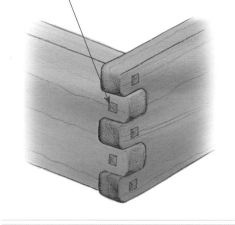

Pins hold joint secure against pulling forces.

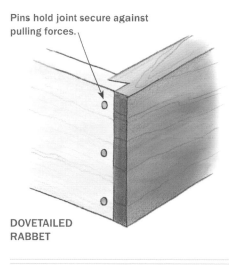

DOVETAILED RABBET

Dovetail Joints

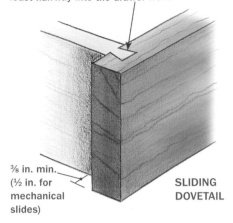

Tail portion, or key, should extend at least halfway into the drawer front.

⅜ in. min. (½ in. for mechanical slides)

SLIDING DOVETAIL

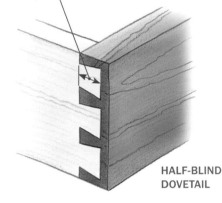

Tails reach about two-thirds of the way into the pin board.

HALF-BLIND DOVETAIL

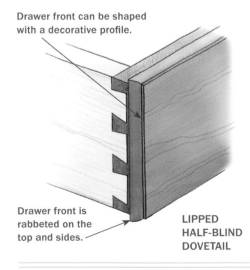

Drawer front can be shaped with a decorative profile.

Drawer front is rabbeted on the top and sides.

LIPPED HALF-BLIND DOVETAIL

Dovetails The sliding dovetail has built-in mechanical strength to keep it together. It offers a quick, strong joinery option, but requires the drawer front to overhang the sides a bit. So it is usually used either on drawers designed with overlay fronts or on flush drawers that ride on mechanical slides or are fitted between wood guides in the case.

Many regard the half-blind version as the king of dovetail joints because of its attractiveness and superior strength. To highlight the craftsmanship, many furniture makers use contrasting woods on the front and sides. Through-dovetails are easier to cut than half-blinds, so the former are the usual choice for the rear corners.

For overlay drawers with excellent strength, use lipped half-blind dovetails. With this joint, the front is rabbeted and joined to the sides with dovetails. Again, through-dovetails are a good option for the rear-corner joints.

Drawers with false fronts

Using false fronts allows you to separate drawer construction from drawer fitting, which ultimately makes both processes easier. With this method, the drawer box is glued up and installed in its opening. Then the false front is cut to size, applied to the box temporarily, adjusted for a perfect reveal (the gap between the drawer and the case),

Nothing beats false fronts when you're using manufactured drawer slides.

At the back

While it's also important to have a sound mechanical joint at the back of the drawer, aesthetics are less of a concern because these corners are rarely seen. For these reasons, rear-corner joints often are different from the front-corner joints. If you are using machine setups to cut the front joinery, however, it makes sense to use those same setups to cut the back joinery.

A rabbeted dado is an easy and effective means of attaching the back to the sides, plus it helps keep the drawer square. Leaving the sides long at the back allows the drawer to be pulled out farther, providing better access.

If you're using sliding dovetails to join the front of the drawer, it's efficient to use the same joints to attach the back. Leaving the sides long at the back will give you access to the full depth of the drawer when it's open.

In traditional dovetailed drawer designs (see the drawings on the facing page), you'll often see through-dovetails at the back. The combination of dovetails at front and back creates a sturdy drawer that will last a lifetime. The pin board typically is cut shorter than the sides to allow the drawer bottom to be slid in after the rest of the box is assembled.

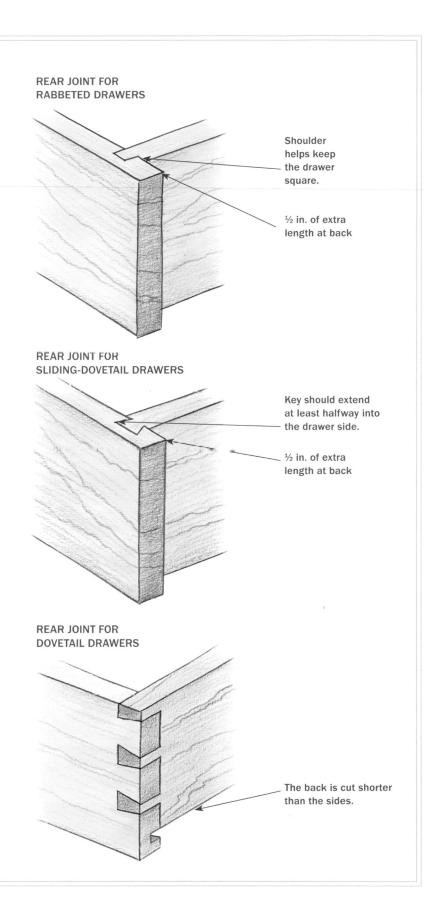

REAR JOINT FOR RABBETED DRAWERS

Shoulder helps keep the drawer square.

½ in. of extra length at back

REAR JOINT FOR SLIDING-DOVETAIL DRAWERS

Key should extend at least halfway into the drawer side.

½ in. of extra length at back

REAR JOINT FOR DOVETAIL DRAWERS

The back is cut shorter than the sides.

Front Joints for False Fronts

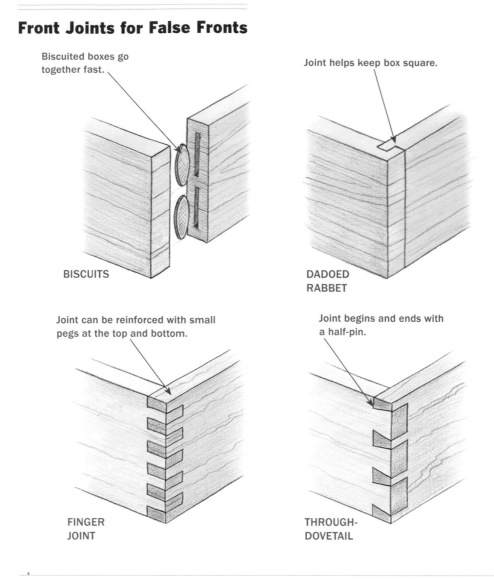

Biscuited boxes go together fast.

BISCUITS

Joint helps keep box square.

DADOED RABBET

Joint can be reinforced with small pegs at the top and bottom.

FINGER JOINT

Joint begins and ends with a half-pin.

THROUGH-DOVETAIL

and then permanently attached to the box. These drawers are ideal for use with manufactured slides, which typically require ½ in. of space on each side of the drawer box.

Biscuits Biscuits offer a quick, strong option to join the sides to the front of a drawer. Once a false front is applied, the end-grain (or plywood) ends of the drawer sides are completely concealed. This joinery system is a good option for kitchen cabinets, built-in units, and utility drawers. Biscuits also

can be used to join the back of the drawer to the sides.

Dadoed rabbet The dadoed rabbet offers a strong mechanical connection at the front of the drawer box, but it's not very attractive. Attaching a false front to the drawer in this case gives the option more appeal. Simple dadoes or tongue-and-rabbet joints are suitable options for the rear joints in this style of drawer construction.

For Drawer Bottoms, Solid Wood Is Elegant, but It Moves

Traditionally, solid-wood panels slide into place after the sides, front, and back of the drawer have been assembled. The back is cut shorter, allowing you to slide the bottom in place, and the bottom is screwed to the back through an elongated hole to allow for wood movement. Building a drawer in this way allows you to take it apart for repairs.

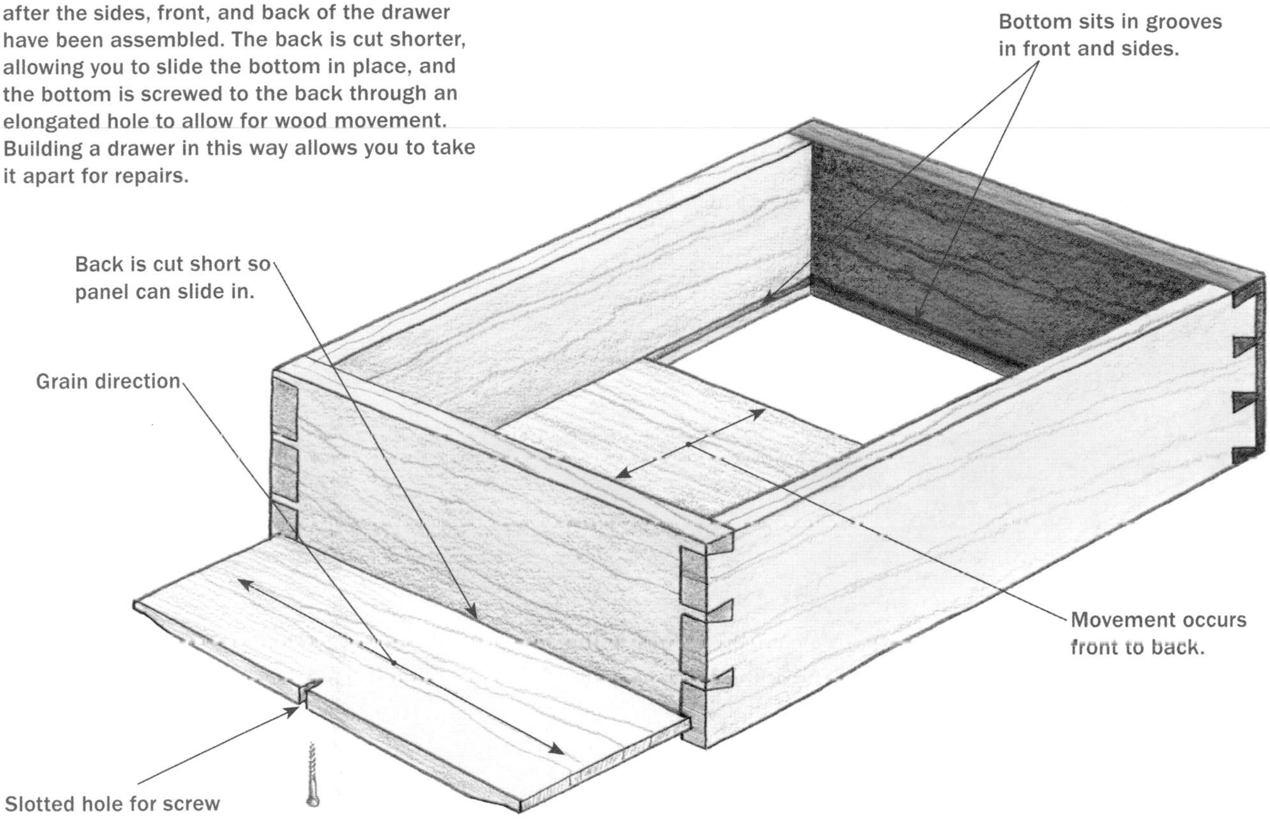

Bottom sits in grooves in front and sides.

Back is cut short so panel can slide in.

Grain direction

Movement occurs front to back.

Slotted hole for screw

BEVEL EDGE
A bevel edge can bind or rattle in its groove if not fit properly. The extra thickness in the middle allows the bottom to carry a heavier load.

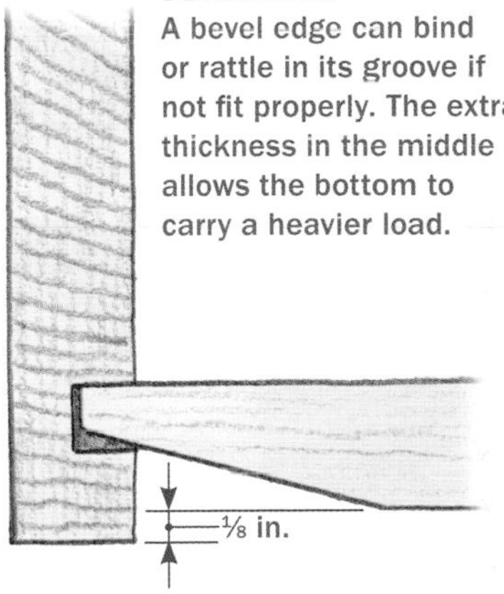

⅛ in.

RAISED PANEL
A raised panel creates a flat on the edge for a better fit in the groove. The flat is usually cut using a router or shaper. The raised area provides a traditional look, and the extra thickness in the middle adds strength.

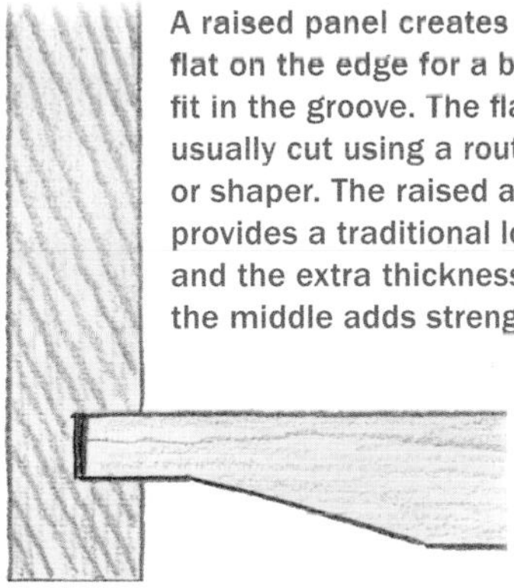

RABBETED
A rabbeted bottom is easier to make, yet offers the same strength as a beveled or raised panel. Watching the gap around the rabbeted edge makes it easy to keep the drawer square during assembly.

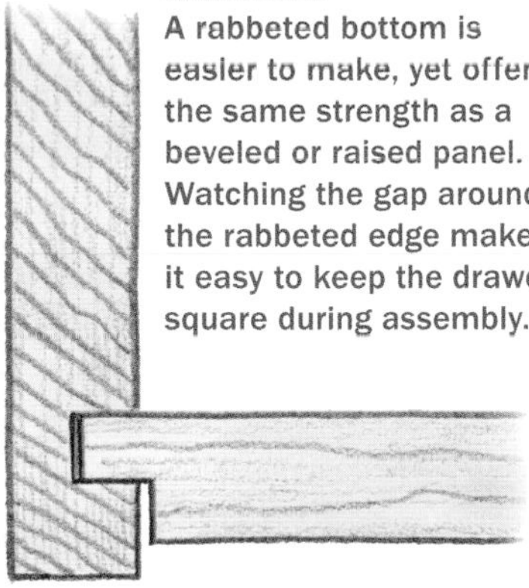

Plywood Is Versatile and Stable

Plywood drawer bottoms are more stable than solid wood and have great strength. A ¼-in.-thick plywood bottom can carry all but the heaviest loads. Plywood bottoms can be slipped in after assembly, just like solid-wood bottoms, or fully housed in grooves, as shown at left. Because of its stability, plywood also can be glued and nailed to the bottom of a plywood drawer box with a false front, a quick, strong option for utility drawers.

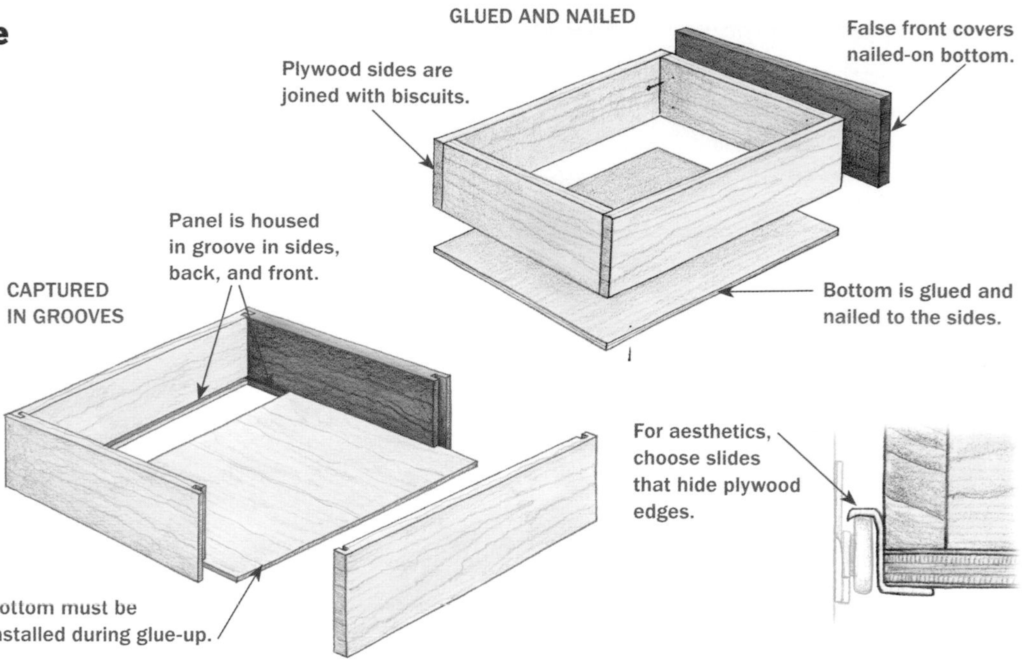

GLUED AND NAILED

Plywood sides are joined with biscuits.

False front covers nailed-on bottom.

Bottom is glued and nailed to the sides.

Panel is housed in groove in sides, back, and front.

CAPTURED IN GROOVES

Bottom must be installed during glue-up.

For aesthetics, choose slides that hide plywood edges.

Finger joint The finger joint is usually hidden behind a false front. It has a series of narrow knuckles that lace together and offer plenty of long-grain glue surfaces. Because the tool setups are the same, if you use finger joints at the front of a drawer, use them at the back, too.

Through-dovetail The angled tails and pins of a through-dovetail create a secure joint that resists pulling and racking forces. If you're cutting through-dovetails by machine (with or without a router jig), it's usually efficient to employ the same joint at the back of the drawer.

Drawer bottoms: fancy or functional

The choice of material and the design of the drawer bottom depend on the style of drawer you are building, whether it's a quick-and-dirty shop drawer or a drawer for an 18th-century secretary.

Both solid wood and plywood are commonly used for drawer bottoms. Solid wood is the traditional choice, and aesthetically, it's hard to beat. But you must allow solid wood to expand and contract with changes in humidity so that it doesn't cause the drawer to bind in its opening (see the top drawing on p. 15).

Plywood is a much more stable choice for a drawer bottom because it does not expand and contract with humidity changes as much as solid wood. Although reproduction builders and a few purists resist plywood bottoms, it's easy to argue their superiority. A plywood bottom can be housed completely in grooves in the sides, back, and front, and glued in place to strengthen the drawer box. Or, it can be slid in from the rear and screwed to the drawer back, or even glued and nailed to the bottom of a drawer box with a false front.

Illustrated Guide to Doors

ANDY RAE

Doors are what we see when we look at a cabinet. Thanks to their relatively large surface area, they're the most visible component in many projects, and they will make a lasting impression if you design them carefully and thoughtfully.

In addition to looking good, doors must function properly. A well-made door opens with little resistance, closes without clatter or fuss, and has a comfortable pull that fits the hand.

Begin by choosing the style of door you want: overlay, rabbeted, or flush. After that, it's a design exercise in proportioning components carefully, choosing the appropriate joinery, and understanding wood movement.

The illustrations on the following pages will help you work out the best door design for whatever project you're planning. This guide covers frame-and-panel doors, the most popular type, used in many furniture styles and periods. Some of the design considerations, however, also apply to slab-style plank doors and veneered doors.

Begin with good proportions

Because doors are the focal point of many pieces, it's important to proportion them so they will work in harmony with each other and with other case components. People frequently make doors and their case openings too wide or, less commonly,

Make It Work Together

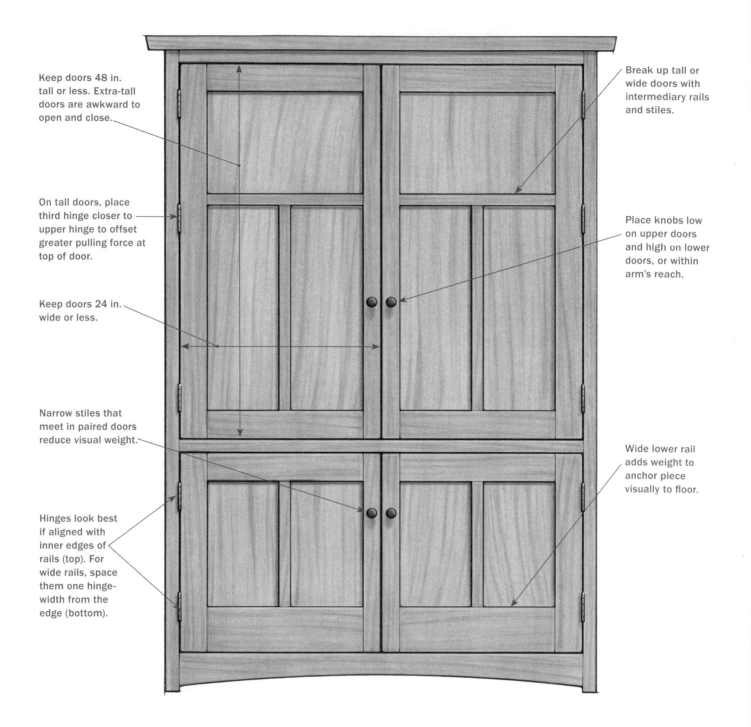

Keep doors 48 in. tall or less. Extra-tall doors are awkward to open and close.

On tall doors, place third hinge closer to upper hinge to offset greater pulling force at top of door.

Keep doors 24 in. wide or less.

Narrow stiles that meet in paired doors reduce visual weight.

Hinges look best if aligned with inner edges of rails (top). For wide rails, space them one hinge-width from the edge (bottom).

Break up tall or wide doors with intermediary rails and stiles.

Place knobs low on upper doors and high on lower doors, or within arm's reach.

Wide lower rail adds weight to anchor piece visually to floor.

Door-Mounting Options

FLUSH DOORS

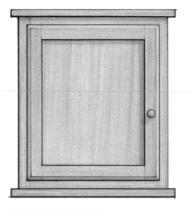

RABBETED DOORS

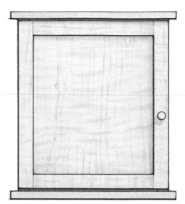

FULL OVERLAY DOORS

too tall. Whenever possible, divide the case opening into reasonable sections and build the doors to suit.

Mounting options

For fine furniture and cabinets, there are three main options: flush, rabbeted, and overlay doors. Each style has some pluses and minuses when it comes to fitting and mounting.

Flush doors are appropriate for both traditional and contemporary furniture. These require the most attention during fitting because the doors hang inside the face of the case. They call for reveals of ¹⁄₁₆ in. or less between the door and case opening.

Rabbeted doors are common in traditional furniture. These sit partially proud of the case, and a rabbet on the back allows them to rest slightly inside the case opening. Because the door gap is concealed, this type is generally the easiest to fit.

Overlay doors are used in contemporary work. Full-overlay doors cover the entire face of the cabinets. Avoid unattractive partial-overlay doors, which are used in factory-made cabinets because they require no fitting.

Options for corner joints

Doors with solid-wood panels get their strength mainly from the corner joints in the frame, while a glued-in plywood or medium density fiberboard (MDF) panel will add considerable rigidity. The time-honored mortise-and-tenon joint is quite common, but the type of joint you use will depend on the look you want and the strength you need, as well as the ease of construction (see the drawing on p. 20).

A haunched tenon is a variation on the basic mortise-and-tenon joint that's easier to make. Both stiles and rails are grooved their full length for the panel. The tenon is cut with a step, or haunch, on one side that fills the groove in the stiles.

A mitered mortise and tenon is another variation on the basic joint. The inside edges of the stiles and rails are mitered after the mortise and tenon are cut. The miter makes it easy to mold a continuous profile along the inside edge.

A miter reinforced with a wood key offers a very strong joint and a contemporary look. Again, the miter makes it easy to run a continuous bead along the inside edge.

Mortise-and-Tenon Options

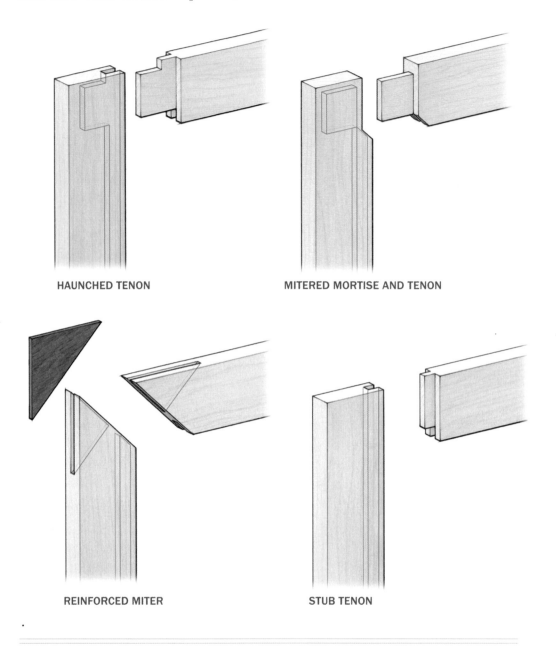

HAUNCHED TENON

MITERED MORTISE AND TENON

REINFORCED MITER

STUB TENON

One more variation on the mortise-and-tenon joint that's very easy to make—a stub tenon. Stiles and rails are grooved their full length, and the tenons are cut to a length equal to the depth of the grooves. A plywood panel glued into the grooves gives the door additional strength.

Frame profiles

A square edge is appropriate for many designs, but edges offer a chance for you to be creative by cutting different profiles or applying a molding. Try a bead ⅛ in. to ¼ in. wide with a ¹⁄₁₆-in. quirk. Cut it on the router table or shaper. It requires a mitered

Frame Profile Options

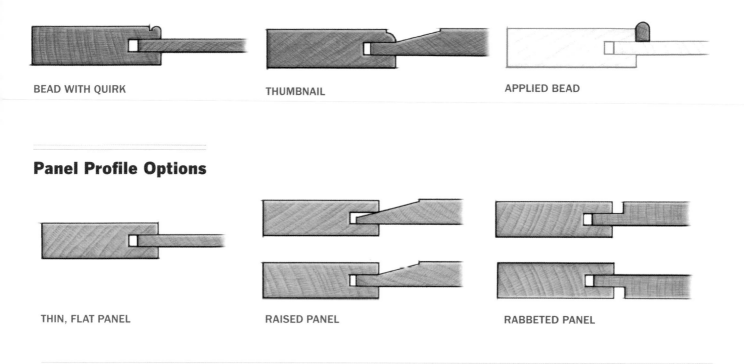

BEAD WITH QUIRK

THUMBNAIL

APPLIED BEAD

Panel Profile Options

THIN, FLAT PANEL

RAISED PANEL

RABBETED PANEL

frame so the bead is continuous. Thumbnails can be quarter-round, quarter-round with fillet (see the top center drawing above), ogee, or other profiles. Shape on a router table or shaper, or by hand. To make an applied bead, shape a ⅛-in. to ¼-in. bead. For all applied beads and moldings, miter the ends, then attach with glue and/or brads.

Panel profiles

Flat panels offer simplicity and are a hallmark of Shaker work. The panel is essentially the same thickness as the groove in the frame. It is made from plywood or MDF, or glued up from narrower solid stock.

Raised panels are more traditional. They have a flat tongue made on a router table or shaper (see the top raised panel drawing above). Alternatively, you can cut the profile on the tablesaw, or form it with a handplane (see the bottom raised panel drawing above).

Rabbets or bevels can be positioned on the back to keep the front plain or they can be profiled on the front only. Both can be designed to be flush with the frame. A rabbeted panel also can be the same thickness as the frame and rabbeted equally front and back.

As a rule, keep the panel flush with or below the surface of the frame.

Hinge options

Well-made hinges installed with care will yield a door that swings smoothly and closes easily. Be sure to select the correct type of hinge for the style of door you're hanging.

Used for overlay and flush doors, a butt hinge requires mortising one or both leaves into the case and door.

Surface hinges are the easiest type to install and are used for flush and rabbeted doors. On rabbeted doors, one leaf is bent to accommodate the offset. Installation is a snap.

Hinge Options

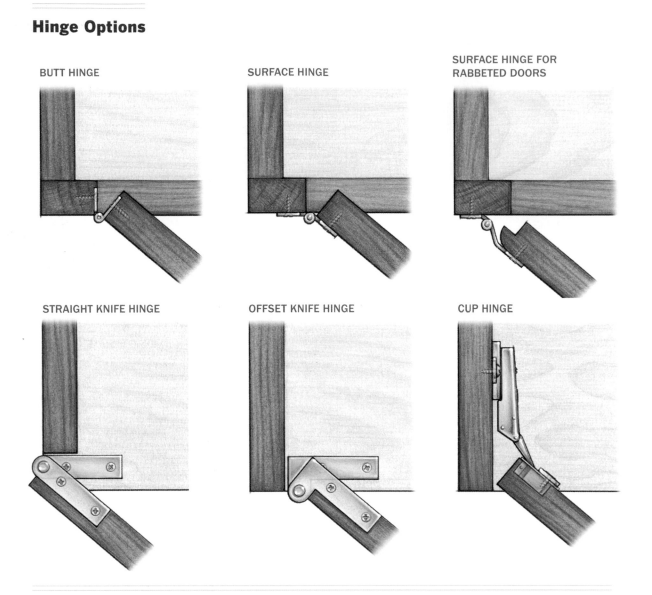

BUTT HINGE

SURFACE HINGE

SURFACE HINGE FOR RABBETED DOORS

STRAIGHT KNIFE HINGE

OFFSET KNIFE HINGE

CUP HINGE

Straight knife hinges are used for overlay doors where the case top and bottom extend over the sides. Offset knife hinges are used for flush doors. Both types of knife hinge require careful mortising of both case and door.

Available for all types of doors, cup hinges are easy to mount in a hole drilled in the back of the door. These hinges give lots of adjustability after the door is mounted.

Whatever you choose, be sure to buy quality hardware. Look for solid castings or extrusions, thick leaves, and knuckles that pivot smoothly without play.

When doors meet

Paired doors are common, offering easier access inside a case. For the tidiest look and one that seals out dust, design the doors with some sort of overlapping element. It's customary to have the right-hand door open first. Also, cut a slight bevel in the edge of one door, to keep it from binding.

When Doors Meet

OPPOSING RABBETS

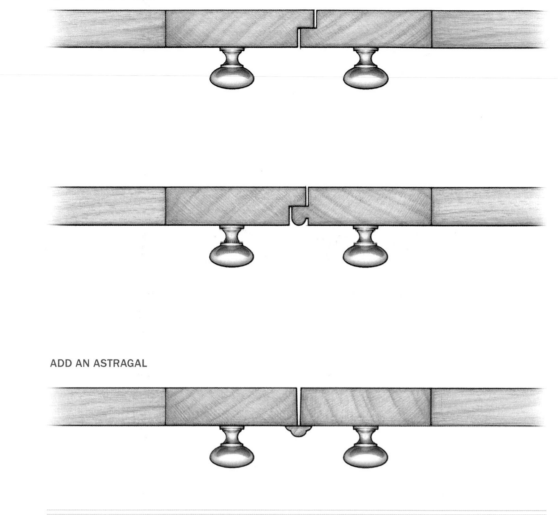

ADD AN ASTRAGAL

Close the gap between doors by cutting matching rabbets in the edges of the stiles. When planning the cabinet, you may need to widen the stile of the door rabbeted on its front (see the top drawing above), so that the stiles appear the same width when closed. Or add an astragal. This is a strip of wood glued either to the face of one door or attached to the back of the captured door. Be sure to cut the astragal a hair short so it won't interfere with the case top or bottom.

Hang It Up

ANISSA KAPSALES

It's common to build a wall cabinet or wall shelf and not give a thought about how to hang it on the wall until it's finished. But planning ahead can give you faster, easier, sturdier, and better-looking ways to hang it up. There are lots of options, ranging from shopmade to store-bought, but here I am concerned only with the ones that are invisible (or nearly so) and, just as important, leave the piece flush against the wall.

The easiest and strongest way to hang things is to build the hanging element, such as a cleat or hanging rail, into the piece. There also are a number of methods that are implemented after construction, such as keyhole slots, hardware, or various manufactured hangers. Often, these methods are fussier because they force you to work awkwardly on a finished piece.

Either way, whether built-in or add-on, it's important to consider the hanging

Keep it on the wall. You need a strong anchor for shelves and wall cabinets.

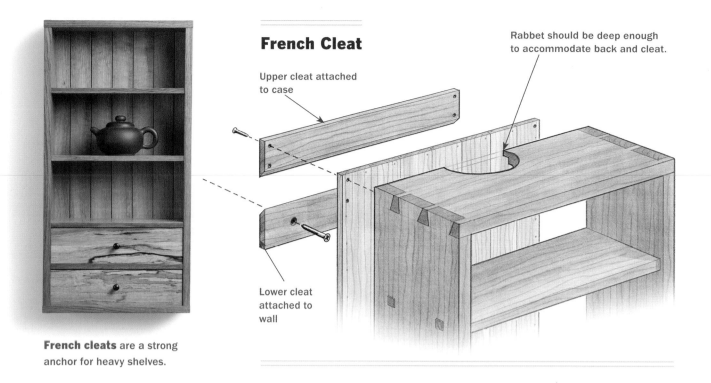

French Cleat

Upper cleat attached to case

Rabbet should be deep enough to accommodate back and cleat.

Lower cleat attached to wall

French cleats are a strong anchor for heavy shelves.

method prior to cutting the first piece of wood because it can influence the thickness of parts, the construction, and the overall design. The following tips for hanging projects are the best I've picked up in my travels as a *Fine Woodworking* editor.

French cleats are strong and easy

A French cleat is simply two pieces of interlocking material, one mounted on the wall and one attached to the furniture. For heavier casework like wall cabinets or closed-back shelves, this is one of the best methods there is. A French cleat can be shopmade or bought (there are extruded-aluminum options on the market); either way the concept is the same. A downside of this method is that you will lose a bit of depth to hide the cleat and keep the piece mounted flush against the wall. You may be tempted

to skimp on the thickness of the cleat, but I wouldn't go much less than ¼ in. thick for a smaller piece and ¾ in. thick for larger, heavier work.

Manufactured cleats

The various extruded-aluminum versions of the French cleat work on the same principle as their shopmade counterparts. However, they are not built into the cabinet but are attached with screws after construction. That doesn't mean you can build the cabinet and forget about the manufactured cleat until afterward. Because you are screwing one part of the cleat to the cabinet, you still have to allow for the cleat's thickness if you want your work to sit flush against the wall. Manufactured cleats do tend to be thinner than the shopmade variety, so you will lose less depth in your cabinet. The cleats are

Make a French cleat

To make a French cleat, simply rip a piece of wood or plywood in half at a 45° angle (1). Screw one cleat through the back and into the sides of the cabinet (2). Secure the second cleat to the wall, lift the cabinet (3), and ease it onto the cleat.

Same concept. Store-bought versions work the same way as shopmade cleats.

going to be carrying all the weight, so they must be attached to a part of the cabinet or shelf that has good structural integrity, such as an internal rail or a solidly constructed back.

Twist on the French cleat

If a cabinet is going to bear a lot of weight, and the planets have aligned so that you can hit just one stud with the wall-mounted side of the cleat, then this T-cleat is perfect. I came across this version at *Fine Woodworking* contributing editor Chris Becksvoort's shop. After he cuts his angled cleats and attaches one of them to the cabinet, he uses a pinned mortise and tenon to join a vertical piece to the horizontal, wall-mounted cleat. This system allows him multiple points of attachment along a single stud.

T-Cleat

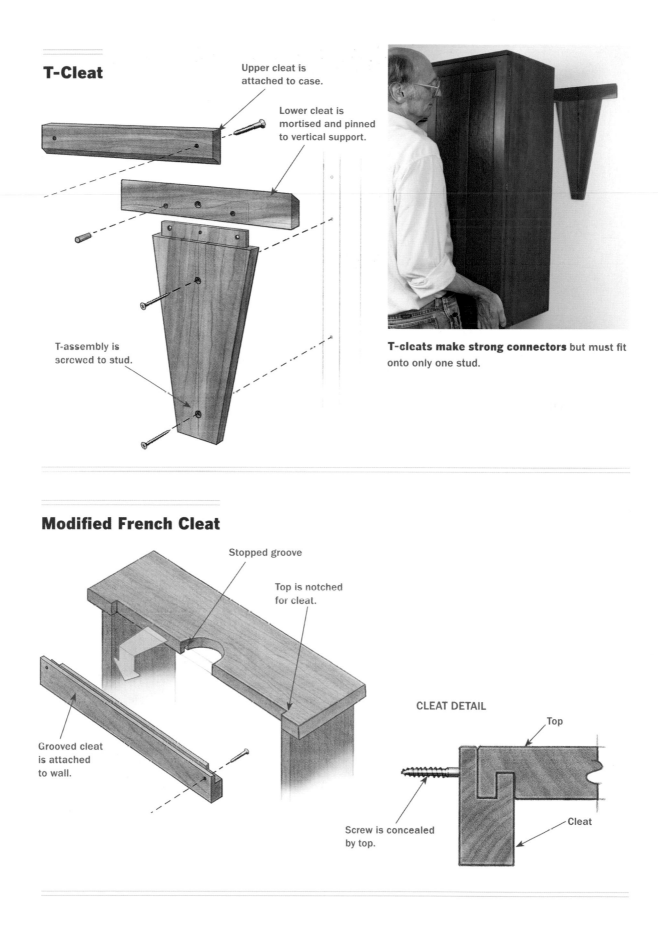

Upper cleat is attached to case.

Lower cleat is mortised and pinned to vertical support.

T-assembly is screwed to stud.

T-cleats make strong connectors but must fit onto only one stud.

Modified French Cleat

Stopped groove

Top is notched for cleat.

Grooved cleat is attached to wall.

CLEAT DETAIL

Top

Screw is concealed by top.

Cleat

Cleat for open-back shelf

This modified French cleat works very well in open-back shelves because the screw holes are concealed. You still must compensate for the thickness of the wall cleat to mount the shelf flush to the wall, so the side and bottom pieces are deeper than the top piece. Because the top of this shelf (see the photo above) overlaps the sides, it gets notched between the side pieces. However, if the carcase were built with dovetails, the sides would extend through the top and notching wouldn't be necessary. The top could just get ripped to a shallower depth (the width of the sides minus the thickness of the cleat) across its width.

Keyholes

You can buy keyhole hangers and install them or make keyhole slots directly on the piece. Either option will allow your shelf or cabinet to hang flush with the wall.

Add a keyhole hanger

Keyhole hangers are sturdy, invisible options that work well for shelves with open backs or wall cabinets where you might not want to sacrifice the space to build in a cleat. Even though you don't install them until after the fact, you have to consider them in the initial construction. In Chris Becksvoort's cherry wall shelf (see the top center photo

Try a modified French cleat on open-back shelves because you'll get the strength of the cleat but the screws will be hidden.

Cut a mortise for the hardware. Mortising the hardware allows the work to hang flat against the wall.

Keyhole hangers are thin so you don't have to leave as much space to include them as you would for a cleat.

Keyhole slots need at least ⅝ in. of material to be strong enough to hold up a shelf.

above), the upright pieces are ¾ in. thick to accommodate the metal hardware and the mortises that are cut underneath the hardware. After scribing around the hanger, freehand rout to a level that equals its thickness, and then use a chisel to clean to the line. Then rout a deeper slot to accept the screw head. Make sure to leave enough wood on the first level to secure the hanger with screws. After the hardware is installed, screws are driven into the wall and the hangers are slotted onto the screws.

Cut keyhole slots in narrow edges

Keyhole slots function the same way as keyhole hardware and also leave your work flush with the wall. They can be used in thinner material than hangers, but they still require at least ⅝ in. of meat in the sides of a cabinet or shelf. The work is slotted so that a screw head in the wall fits in at the bottom of the slot and gets confined at the top. You'll need a special bit and a plunge router, using an edge guide to guide the router, or using a template and collar. The trick is to plunge down, run the groove, back up, and come back up in the same place you started. For this reason, I like to use a template and collar (see the top left photo on p. 30) or clamp a start/stop block at the beginning of the cut.

A specialized bit for keyhole slots. Keyhole slots don't require additional hardware, but they do require a bit with a round cutter at the tip as well as a cutter on the shank.

Slots are added after construction. A router template (shopmade or store-bought) can be clamped to the workpiece (left). A plunge router equipped with a guide bushing and keyhole bit rides in the template to cut the slot (right).

Screw it in

If you're not concerned about screw holes or you're planning to cover them up, consider a hanging rail or simply screwing the shelf directly to the wall.

Hanging rails are simple and strong

An internal hanging rail should be mortised into the cabinet during construction. The rail sits inside and unobtrusively at the top and is screwed through to mount the cabinet directly to the wall. You can plug the screw holes with removable plugs to maintain

This tea-stained and milk-painted wall cabinet was hung by screwing through an internal hanging rail into the wall.

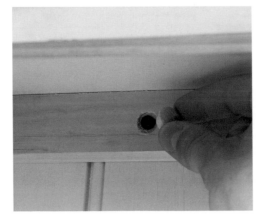

Cover up screw holes. Counterbore the screw holes and insert removable plugs to cover the screw heads.

Hide the Screws

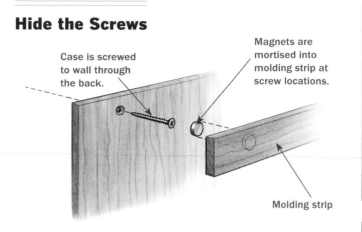

Case is screwed to wall through the back.

Magnets are mortised into molding strip at screw locations.

Molding strip

Cover unsightly screw holes with a magnetized molding strip. Tuck it up against the top of the cabinet.

easy access in the future. But if the cabinet is mounted high enough and things are placed inside, you probably won't see the screws anyway.

Go right through the back

Even easier than an internal hanging rail is this method of screwing through the back of the cabinet and concealing the screw holes with a magnetized molding strip. This method is very straightforward and the magnetized strip looks like a construction detail. Despite its simplicity, this method should be carefully planned and executed. First, the back has to be strong enough to hold the weight of the cabinet and anything that will be in it. It's best to use a back that is at least ¼ in. thick, and glue and nail or screw it in place for extra support. The cabinet back shouldn't be recessed from the back edges of the carcase or it could separate when you screw it into the wall. Keep the screws near the top of the cabinet so the wood strip can be discreetly bumped against the top, and mortise small rare-earth magnets into the back side of the strip, lining them up with the screw heads.

When the top is hidden

Not entirely invisible, these metal hangers (called "rigid hangers") are screwed or

Above eye level. The ideal situation for rigid hangers is a cabinet like this one. The crown molding is above head height and also extends beyond the top of the case, concealing the hangers.

Hollow-wall anchors

When screwing into the wall, the best scenario is that you'll hit two studs and be done with it, but that is rare. You'll be lucky to hit one. Since you don't want to tear apart the wall to insert 2x4 blocks between studs, you'll have to use hollow-wall anchors. Options range from expansion anchors and mollies to augers and toggles. Although toggle bolts are generally strongest, I prefer to sacrifice some strength and use augers. They are still strong, but easier to install precisely. The wings on toggles require an oversize hole in the wall, and there can be play as you tighten and position them. Augers are simply screwed into the wallboard, then screws are secured into the anchor. I've used auger-type anchors rated from 15 lb. to 100 lb. for shear strength. But that varies by brand and depends on the thickness of the wallboard, so be sure to check the manufacturer's specifications.

Strength varies widely. Different types of anchors vary in strength and ease of installation. Manufacturers can provide stats on the tensile strength (or pullout) and shear strength (or downward pull) of each.

Rigid hangers extend above the top of the cabinet or shelf.

mortised into the upper parts of a cabinet or shelf and have a keyhole or a hole that extends beyond the top and fits over screws mounted on the wall. These hangers work best on pieces that have a decorative molding and are hung well above eye level. As with most hanging devices, make sure you have enough structural integrity to mount them securely to the workpiece. You can mortise the hanger into the piece. Even if you don't, it is thin enough (less than 1⁄16 in.) that the cabinet or shelf will sit nearly flush against the wall.

Do an About-Face on Cabinets

STEVE LATTA

This small but classic bookcase is one of my favorite projects. The finished piece is practical and attractive, and for the fledgling woodworker it presents a great introduction to face-frame case construction.

A face frame on a case piece serves a couple of different roles. It improves how the piece looks, letting you hide through-dadoes and change proportions to make the front of the piece appear more substantial and formal. And, if you're adding doors, it can

For better cabinet pieces, start with the face frame, not the box.

A Case Study

Building a case frame-first lends itself well to the practice of fitting parts to a piece as you build it, a process known as "verify in field." The face frame becomes a template for sizing and locating other major components, so do not pre-cut parts to final size for this bookcase, or any project for that matter.

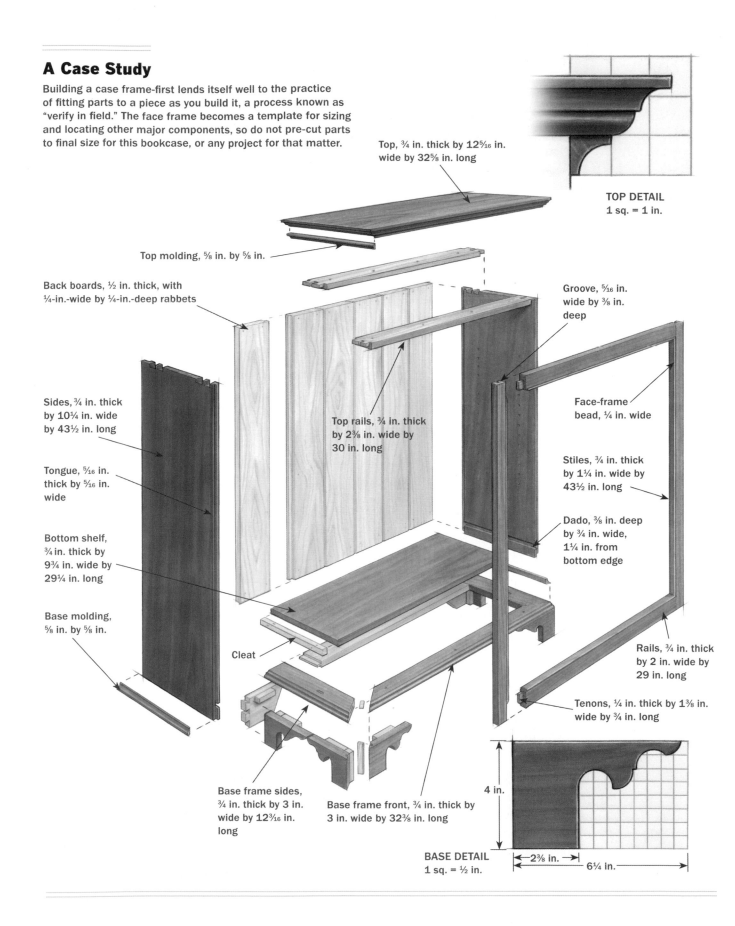

Top, ¾ in. thick by 12⁵⁄₁₆ in. wide by 32⅝ in. long

TOP DETAIL
1 sq. = 1 in.

Top molding, ⅝ in. by ⅝ in.

Back boards, ½ in. thick, with ¼-in.-wide by ¼-in.-deep rabbets

Groove, ⁵⁄₁₆ in. wide by ⅜ in. deep

Sides, ¾ in. thick by 10¼ in. wide by 43½ in. long

Top rails, ¾ in. thick by 2⅜ in. wide by 30 in. long

Face-frame bead, ¼ in. wide

Tongue, ⁵⁄₁₆ in. thick by ⁵⁄₁₆ in. wide

Stiles, ¾ in. thick by 1¼ in. wide by 43½ in. long

Bottom shelf, ¾ in. thick by 9¾ in. wide by 29¼ in. long

Dado, ⅜ in. deep by ¾ in. wide, 1¼ in. from bottom edge

Base molding, ⅝ in. by ⅝ in.

Cleat

Rails, ¾ in. thick by 2 in. wide by 29 in. long

Tenons, ¼ in. thick by 1⅜ in. wide by ¾ in. long

Base frame sides, ¾ in. thick by 3 in. wide by 12³⁄₁₆ in. long

Base frame front, ¾ in. thick by 3 in. wide by 32⅜ in. long

4 in.

BASE DETAIL
1 sq. = ½ in.

2⅜ in. — 6¼ in.

Frame is the foundation

Build the case by first assembling the face frame (1). Next, rabbet the sides into grooves in the back of the frame (2). With the frame dry-fitted to the sides, mark out and fit the bottom shelf and top rails (3). After gluing up the case and attaching the frame, size and attach the top and base (4).

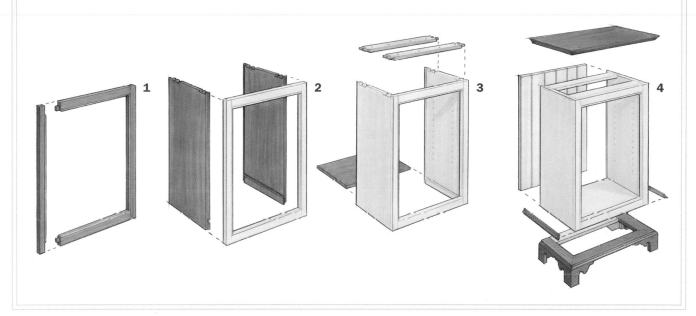

A simple bookcase is easy to build using the face-frame-first method.

help keep the opening square and allows a good mounting surface for the hinges.

Like anything else in woodworking, though, there's more than one way to get the job done. Many furniture makers build the case first and then assemble and attach the face frame. I take a different approach. My early woodshop training was in commercial cabinetry, where the practice was to build the frame first. I do it that way for fine furniture, too, because it offers several advantages.

First, building the frame at the outset gives me the freedom to alter its dimensions slightly to fix any tearout or minor mistakes in its construction. For instance, this frame is decorated with a bead around its inner edge with miters in the corners that can be easy to miscut. I'd lose the flexibility to make an easy fix if I were building the frame to fit an already glued-up case.

Second, I like joining the face frame to the case with strong and positive tongue-and-groove joinery as opposed to just gluing the frame in place. Assembling the face frame before building the case makes it easier to locate that joinery. I like that positive connection because the assembled frame helps align the whole assembly during glue-up of the case, simplifying the process and helping to ensure that it goes together squarely.

If you've never tried the face-frame-first method, read on. This handsome bookcase project will illustrate all of the advantages.

Put your best face forward

The face frame on this cabinet is decorated with a ¼-in. bead that runs around the inside edge and is mitered at the corners. I cut this bead at the router table while the stock is still wide and long, so that any bead marred by tearout, snipe, or other mistakes can be cut away and redone.

Afterward, rip the frame members extra wide and run them through the planer on edge to a finished width that is ¹⁄₃₂ in. greater than called for in the drawing on p. 34. Later, after the case and frame are glued up, you'll plane away this extra material to bring the frame flush with the case sides.

Milling trick. After cutting the bead on the rails and stiles, run the pieces on edge through the planer to guarantee consistent widths.

Cut clean joinery. Because the case is not yet constructed, any problems with the corner joints can be corrected by recutting them and making the frame slightly smaller.

Glue up the frame. Check that the frame is square and flat. The joints should come together cleanly with no gaps.

As I mentioned, mitering the beaded corners on the frame can be challenging because it's possible to miscut by a fraction and wind up with a gappy miter. If that happens, simply cut the miter again and recut the corresponding parts to match. You'll end up with a slightly shorter or narrower frame, but that won't be an issue since my process ensures that the case will fit the frame.

If, instead, I messed up a miter while trying to fit the frame to an already assembled case, I wouldn't have room for that sort of adjustment. My only choice would be to waste time and stock milling up new frame parts.

Once the miters are cut, you can cut the joinery for the face frame and then glue up the frame. When gluing up, be sure to clamp carefully to avoid twist, and check diagonal measurements to ensure that the frame stays square.

It's impossible to go wrong on the case

Here's a great feature of this approach. Notice how the process ensures a perfectly sized case. Because the case isn't built yet, and the parts are still oversize, I can now rabbet the front edge of the case sides, cut grooves in the rear of the frame stiles, and then dry-fit the two to find the exact length of all the case's crosspieces.

Also, this case-to-frame joinery is easier to execute than locating biscuits on a face frame, and it's much stronger and more manageable to glue up than a simple butt joint between the case and frame.

Still, it's important to locate the grooves in the back of the frame carefully so the frame ends up ⅓₂-in. proud of each side, for planing flush later. To ensure a snug fit and accurate placement of the groove, I cut test joints in scrap stock.

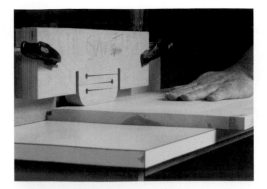

Rabbet the case side.
Rabbet the front of the case sides to create a tongue for the face frame, but leave the sides wide so you can trim away any mistakes. Putting the cutter above the work ensures consistent thickness for the tongue, as long as there is a hold-down pushing down on the workpiece.

Groove the face frame.
Cut test grooves in a piece of scrap (above) to locate the groove accurately. When this is done, the frame should overlap the rabbeted side by $\frac{1}{32}$ in. (above right). Now cut the grooves in the frame (right). Clamp a piece of long stock to a sawhorse or table to help support the workpiece.

With the case-to-frame joinery cut, you can use the frame to find the exact sizes of all the case parts, and locate the dadoes in them. After squaring the bottom of each side, dry-fit them to the face frame, mark their height and width, and then cut them to size on the tablesaw.

The face frame also serves as a reference for sizing and locating the bottom shelf and the rails across the top. With the sides cut to size and once again dry-fitted into the face frame,

I locate the dadoes that will hold the bottom shelf, to ensure that it ends up perfectly level with the frame's lower rail. Once these dadoes are cut, I go ahead and rabbet the back edges of the case sides to accept the back. Then, I dry-fit the frame and sides again to measure for the bottom shelf's length (see the right photo on the facing page). When the shelf is cut to length and dry-fitted, you can mark and then rip it so it ends at the rabbet.

Locate the dadoes in the case sides. To ensure that the bottom shelf ends up level with the bottom rail of the face frame, use a combination square to pick up the width of the rail.

Transfer the dimension. Put the square against the outside of the dado set to position the rip fence. You can trust that it's right.

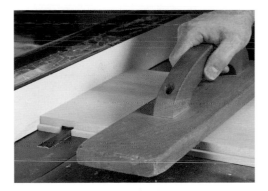

Dado with no doubts. Verify the cut's location in a test piece, then cut the dado. Use a wide push paddle with a cleat in the rear to guide the workpiece.

Dry-fit and measure. Use a tape measure or, better yet, two overlapping rulers to measure between the dado bottoms for the precise length of the shelf.

The screw rails that support the case's top are joined to the sides with a pair of shouldered through-dovetails at each end. Working with the frame, sides, and bottom all dry-fitted allows me to quickly fit the shoulders very accurately with no measuring or even marking.

I start with the rails about 1/16 in. longer than the outside width of the case. This will leave about a 1/32-in. overhang on each side that will be easily pared with a chisel.

Using a miter gauge and the saw's fence, make a shoulder cut on each end that you know is too short. At the bandsaw, remove

Cut with confidence. Because you used the face frame to position the sides, you know this shelf will fit perfectly.

Leave them oversize. With the rails ¹⁄₁₆ in. longer than the width of the case, Latta begins cutting the shoulders.

Shoulders first. Working again with the rest of the case dry-fitted, Latta can cut the shoulders accurately. He removes material in small increments from both ends until the shoulders drop snugly between the case sides.

just enough of both cheeks to let you butt against the shoulder for test-fitting. Now you can sneak up on the fit by moving the fence farther away from the blade in small increments and recutting the shoulders until the rail drops in place. For accuracy's sake, make sure you are fitting right behind the face frame. Once the shoulder cuts are established, cut the cheeks using a tenoning jig or a high fence. Now you can cut the tails and easily lay out the mortises in the tops of the sides (see the top left photo on the facing page).

As a last step before glue-up, drill the shelf-pin holes.

One part determines the next. With the shouldered dovetails cut, Latta marks their mating sockets in the top of the case sides.

The frame simplifies glue-up, too

The case glue-up is another stage where having an assembled frame is a distinct advantage. Keeping the case parts together during glue-up can be a challenging exercise in positioning cauls and shifting clamps. But the tongue-and-groove connection to the frame helps to keep everything aligned and eliminates a lot of fussing. I start by dry-fitting the top screw rails in place and then gluing the bottom into the case sides (see the photo below left). Then I immediately dry-fit the frame to the sides to help keep them parallel before putting the assembly in clamps. Then I glue in the screw rails at the top. When the glue is dry, I remove the face frame, apply glue, and reattach it to the case.

Dry-fit the top to glue up the bottom. With the top rails holding the sides in place, Latta brushes glue into the dadoes that will hold the bottom shelf. Cleats that allow for cross-grain movement will be added later to reinforce this joint.

Add the frame, too. Dry-fitting the frame helps square the assembly and hold it rigid. With the frame in place, you can clamp the sides tight to the bottom.

Now glue in the top rails. Leave the dry-fitted frame in place.

When the assembly comes out of clamps, I use a plane, scraper, and sanding block to bring the face-frame stiles flush with the case sides (see the bottom photo below). Check often to make sure the corners stay square, especially at the bottom where the cove molding will be attached. When this work is done, you are ready to add the base and top.

Glue on the frame. When the bottom shelf and top rails are dry, remove the frame, apply glue, and clamp it in place.

Trim to fit. Use a block plane or scraper to remove the excess frame stock that overhangs the sides of the case. Everything will be square and perfect now, and ready for the crown moldings and base.

A Portable Book Rack

GREGORY PAOLINI

Years ago, while researching American Arts and Crafts designs, I took an immediate liking to Gustav Stickley's No. 74 book rack. It's shorter than most bookcases, with slats that form a V-shaped trough to hold books spine up. Its D-shaped handholds make it easy to move.

I've made a dozen racks based on that design, from small desktop versions to extra-tall ones that hold compact discs and DVDs. I've also modified Stickley's design. Simple through-tenons replace the wedged tenons. I added a second V-shaped trough in the middle to make the rack more functional, and I tapered the end panels, reflecting the look of the Roycroft designs that I favor. Despite the changes, the book rack retains its Arts and Crafts character. This version, made from quartersawn white oak, is sized to sit between a couple Morris chairs.

Make the end panels and router template

Since the end panels are the focal point, you want boards with maximum figure. Use single wide boards if you have them, or edge-glue narrower boards.

While the panels are drying, make a router template from ¼-in. medium-density fiberboard (MDF) or plywood, which you'll use to cut slots for the shelf mortises.

(continued on p. 46)

Book Rack Plans

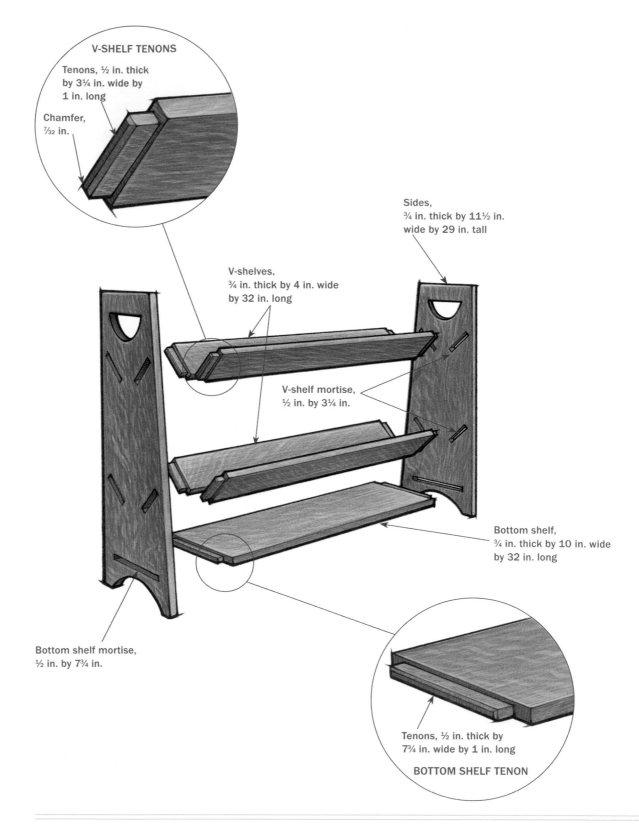

V-SHELF TENONS

Tenons, ½ in. thick by 3¼ in. wide by 1 in. long

Chamfer, ⁷⁄₃₂ in.

Sides, ¾ in. thick by 11½ in. wide by 29 in. tall

V-shelves, ¾ in. thick by 4 in. wide by 32 in. long

V-shelf mortise, ½ in. by 3¼ in.

Bottom shelf, ¾ in. thick by 10 in. wide by 32 in. long

Bottom shelf mortise, ½ in. by 7¾ in.

Tenons, ½ in. thick by 7¾ in. wide by 1 in. long

BOTTOM SHELF TENON

SIDE TEMPLATE

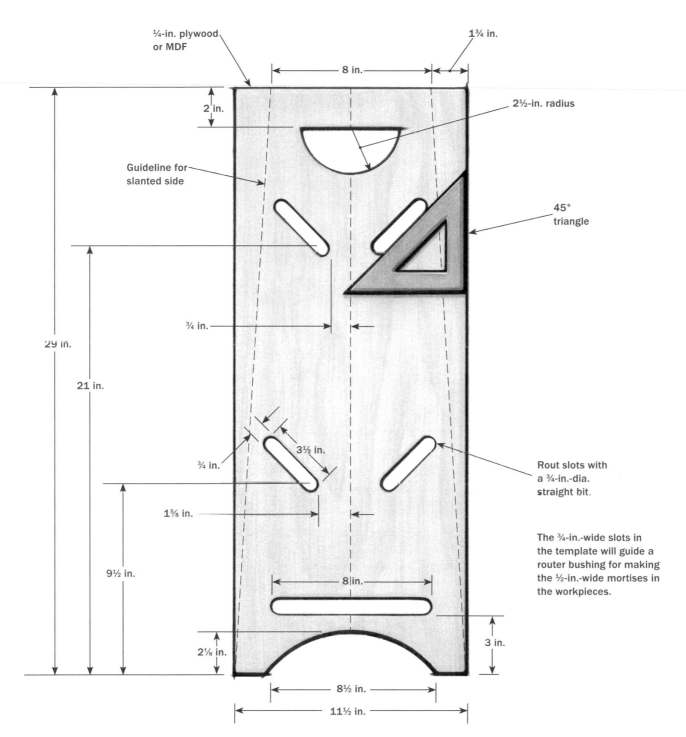

¼-in. plywood or MDF

1¾ in.

8 in.

2½-in. radius

2 in.

Guideline for slanted side

45° triangle

¾ in.

29 in.

21 in.

Rout slots with a ¾-in.-dia. straight bit.

¾ in.

3½ in.

1⅝ in.

The ¾-in.-wide slots in the template will guide a router bushing for making the ½-in.-wide mortises in the workpieces.

9½ in.

8 in.

3 in.

2⅛ in.

8½ in.

11½ in.

Making the Template

Lay out the slots. Align the template and the triangle against a straightedge clamped to the bench to draw the shelf outlines.

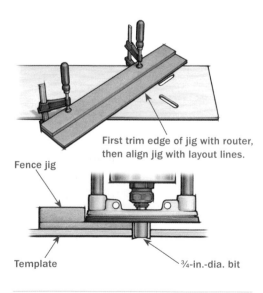

Make the cutouts. Use a straight bit and a fence jig to cut the ¾-in. slots for the shelf mortises. Use a jigsaw for the other cutouts.

First trim edge of jig with router, then align jig with layout lines.

Fence jig

Template

¾-in.-dia. bit

The template (see the drawing on p. 45) simplifies construction in several ways. It locates the shelf mortises, of course. And because I clamp the template to the inside face of one end piece and the outside face of the other, it ensures that the mortises will line up. When laying out the slots in the template, all you have to do is draw the dimensions for the ¾-in.-thick shelves and cut a slot that wide. When using those slots to cut the through-mortises, use a bit and guide bushing. The offset between bit and bushing equals the width of the tenon shoulders. I get a mortise the right width, in the right location.

To avoid tearout when routing through-mortises, I work from one face toward the middle, without popping out the other side. So I rout the bulk of the mortises with the guide bushing, then use a flush-trimming bit from the other side to finish them cleanly.

Make the template 11½ in. wide by 29 in. long (see the drawing on p. 45). Draw the panel side tapers, handle, and lower arch. Then draw rectangles represent-ing the full size of the ends of the narrow V-shelves and the wide bottom shelf. With the template drawn, draw layout lines ¼ in. from each end of the V-shelf rectangles. For the bottom shelf, draw layout lines 1 in. from the ends. These define the starting and stopping points for the shelf mortises. To cut the mortise slots, clamp a shopmade fence jig flush with the long side of each shelf outline and plunge cut from one line to the next with a router and a ¾-in. bit. Cut out the handle and bottom arch with a jigsaw, then smooth the curves and clean up the sawmarks with sandpaper.

Secret to Clean Through-Mortises

INITIAL CUTS
Begin cutting the shelf mortises with a plunge router equipped with a ¼-in.-dia. spiral upcut bit and a ½-in. guide bushing. Use the same setup to make the curved cutouts. Make these cuts only about ⅝ in. deep; don't cut through the work at this stage.

FINAL CUTS
Finish the mortises and other cutouts with a ⅜-in. flush-trimming bit, working from the opposite face.

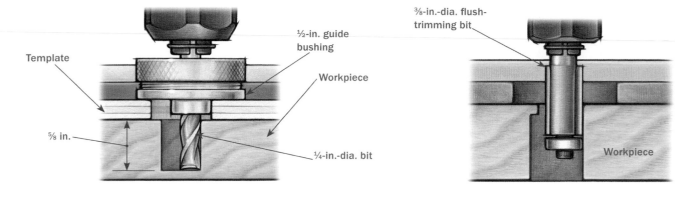

Template

½-in. guide bushing

Workpiece

⅝ in.

¼-in.-dia. bit

⅜-in.-dia. flush-trimming bit

Workpiece

Mill the oak and cut the mortises

Next, I mill all the oak shelves to size and cut the glued-up end panels to length. However, I won't taper the panels until I've finished making all the cutouts with the router.

I make the mortises and cutouts on one panel at a time. Rather than clamping them together and cutting everything at once, I set up the template so that the panels are oriented as copies, not mirror images. In other words, the template goes on the outside face of the left-hand panel but on the inside face of the right-hand panel.

Register the template to the side and bottom of the end panel. You can use a long scrap of wood as a fence to help align the template with the side. Clamp the assembly to the bench and mark a small dot on the bottom of the right foot. You'll use that mark to reference how you laid out the panel.

Set up the router and bushing. The ¾-in.-wide slots in the template will produce a ½-in.-wide mortise in the oak, using a ¼-in. spiral bit and a ½-in. bushing. You could also

use a ⅜-in. bit and a ⅝-in. bushing. However, the smaller bit leaves a tiny ridge dead-center in the groove, which comes in handy later on.

Rout the outlines for the D-shaped handle, the lower arch, and the shelf mortises in several passes. Don't cut all the way through. When the cuts are about ⅝ in. deep, stop and remove the template. Use a jigsaw to remove most of the waste from the handle and the lower arch.

Drill a hole through each shelf mortise. This is where you can use that ridge left by the ¼-in. bit. I like to use it to center a 1⁄16-in.-dia. pilot hole. Then I flip the panel over and enlarge the pilot hole with a 13⁄32-in. bit. This gives me a starting place for the router bit I use next.

Flip the panel over, and finish all the cuts with a ⅜-in. flush-trimming bit. I chuck the bit in a laminate trimmer. It's easy to control and lets me easily see what I'm doing.

These extra steps guarantee that you won't have any tearout. Square up the mortises with a chisel, working from each face toward the middle to avoid tearout. Finish the panels

Rout the mortises to partial depth. Use a guide bushing for initial cuts. Clamp the template to the workpiece.

by tapering the sides on the bandsaw, cutting just to the waste side of the line. I clean up the cuts with a router, using my shopmade edge guide and a straight bit.

Cut the tenons on the tablesaw

The through-tenons on the shelves project ¼ in. from the side panels. They have narrow shoulders on their wide faces, and deep shoulders on the sides. The shoulders hide some imperfections and make glue-up much easier. I cut the tenons on the tablesaw, defining the shoulders with a combination blade to minimize tearout, then switching to

a stacked dado set to finish (see the top left and center left photos on p. 50).

You should purposely make the shoulder cuts a hair too deep, which prevents a ridge at the inside corner that you'd have to clean out later.

Trade the combination blade for a stacked dado set to finish the tenons. Cut the wide cheeks first. Set the blade low and raise it gradually through a series of cuts to sneak up on the proper tenon thickness. Test the fit after each cut. Once that first tenon fits the mortise just right, cut the rest. Follow the same procedure to cut all the short cheeks.

Starter holes for the next step. Drill a hole to allow the flush-trimming bit to enter the mortise. Start with a small pilot hole to locate the center. To prevent blowout, follow with a larger bit from the other side.

Flip the work and finish with a flush-trimming bit. To clean up the D-shaped handle and the cutout at the foot, cut away most of the waste with a jigsaw, then use the same bit to smooth the edge.

Square up the corners. Cut away the waste in the corners with a chisel. Chop about halfway down, then flip the work and finish by paring from the opposite face toward the center.

Define the shoulders. Use a combination blade to make the initial cuts for the tenon shoulders. Make these cuts about 1/32 in. deeper than the tenon, to define the shoulders cleanly.

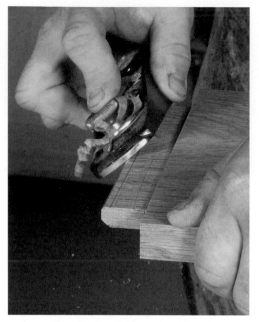

Chamfer the tenon ends. Use a block plane to chamfer the portion of each tenon that will be proud of the side pieces, working to a layout line. To minimize tearout, plane the wide cheeks first, then the narrow ends.

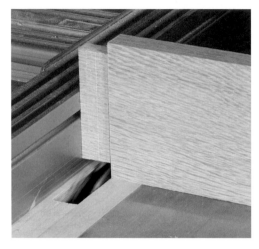

Finish with a dado set. Use a stacked dado set to cut away the waste on each tenon. Check the first tenon often against its mortise to creep up on the right blade height.

Next, chamfer the ends of the tenons. Mark a line 7/32 in. from the ends, then plane to that line at roughly a 45° angle. Plane the long edges first, then plane the short edges (see the photo above right).

Finally, soften the remaining sharp edges of the shelves and side panels with a 1/4-in. roundover bit in the router.

Fit and finish

Dry-fit the piece. The tenons should slip into their mortises with hand pressure. If you need a mallet, the joints are too tight and you'll need to pare down the tenons with a shoulder plane or a coarse file. Smooth the pieces with a random-orbit sander, finishing with P180-grit. Then hand-sand all the pieces with P180-grit paper, working with the grain, to minimize any sanding swirls.

I like to do some of the finishing before assembly, when the pieces are easy to handle.

The result. You should have tenons with even shoulders, smooth cheeks, and a nice fit.

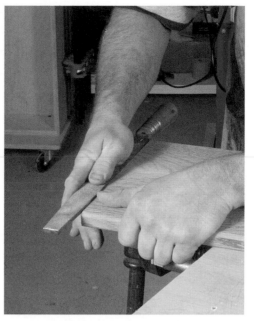

Fine-tune the fit. The tenons should fit into the mortises with hand pressure. At the end, you may need to remove a small amount of excess with a coarse file (above) or a shoulder plane.

Dye, then stain. A brownish dye, followed by a darker oil stain, produces a finish that's very close to fumed oak. Mask the tenons to keep finish off glue surfaces (left). When applying the finish, work carefully to keep the stain out of the mortises (right).

Glue, then shellac. To reduce squeezeout, put most of the glue on the tenons and only a dab in the mortises. When the glue has cured, apply several coats of thinned shellac. As a final step, rub out the finish.

To keep finish off the tenons, I wrap them with ½-in. masking tape.

For a simple finish, I like Minwax® Early American 230 stain followed by clear shellac or varnish, which looks remarkably like one of Stickley's original finishes.

After the stain has dried, glue up the piece. If you get any squeeze-out, let it dry, then peel it off.

In keeping with the Arts and Crafts tradition, I use shellac as a topcoat. I typically brush on six or seven coats of Zinsser® SealCoat® thinned to a 1-lb. cut. After the shellac has cured, I rub out the piece with mineral oil and 0000 steel wool, giving the piece the satin sheen typical of this style of furniture. The finish should provide plenty of protection for a few generations of readers.

Quick, Sturdy Bookcase

MARTIN MILKOVITS

In my home, bookcases show up in every room, serving not only as places to store our growing collection of books, but also as places to display art and other items of interest. This bookcase is a versatile piece, big enough to hold a good number of books and/or collectibles while small enough to fit in almost any room.

The design is understated, with bracket feet and gentle curves along the tops of the sides, and maple back boards contrasting softly with butternut sides and shelves. The back boards are shiplapped to allow for wood movement.

The shelves are attached to the sides with sliding dovetails, which are often used to connect cabinet tops to bottoms, to join vertical partitions to shelves, to attach molding to case sides, to connect breadboard ends to tabletops, and to attach drawer fronts to sides. Sliding dovetails provide a mechanical connection that will never pull apart. But that same quality also makes the joint difficult to assemble, especially with wide parts, so I taper the joint to make the glue-up go smoothly. In this case, I also stopped the dovetails for a clean look on the front of the piece.

Why taper the dovetail?

A sliding dovetail has two parts: the slot and the dovetail key. Here, the slots are routed into the case sides, and the keys are cut on the ends of the shelf. When you use this joint

in wide stock, binding is a common headache during glue-up. The joint goes halfway home, then the glue makes the wood swell and the joint seizes. That's why I taper the joint slightly toward the front of the case. The taper—cut on one side of the slot and on the

Anatomy of a Sturdy Bookcase

This butternut-and-maple bookcase can hold a heavy load of books. The tapered sliding dovetails that connect the shelves to the sides create a powerful wedged joint and eliminate the need for clamps during assembly. All of the parts are made of ¾-in.-thick stock, except for the back boards (see detail).

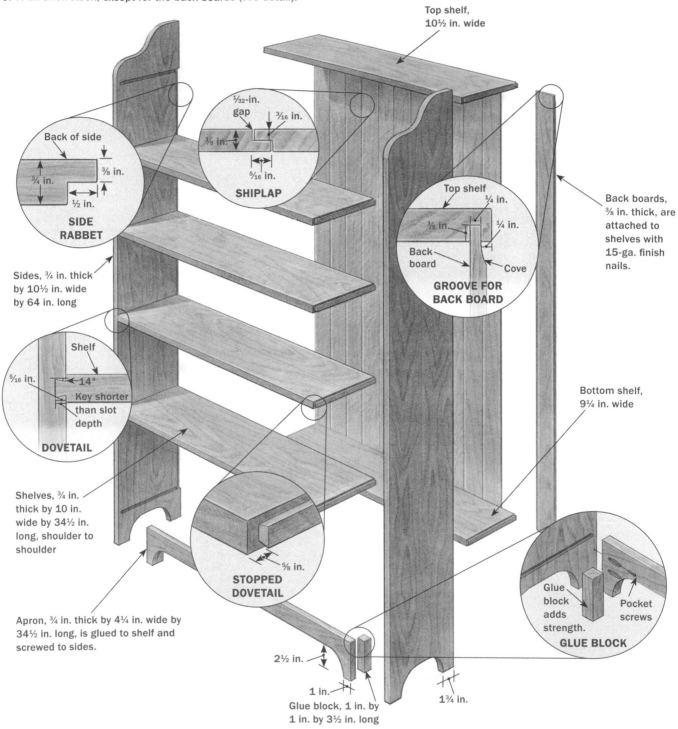

Top shelf, 10½ in. wide

Back of side

¾ in.

⅜ in.

½ in.

SIDE RABBET

Sides, ¾ in. thick by 10½ in. wide by 64 in. long

1/32-in. gap

⅜ in.

3/16 in.

5/16 in.

SHIPLAP

Top shelf

¼ in.

⅜ in.

¼ in.

Back board

Cove

GROOVE FOR BACK BOARD

Back boards, ⅜ in. thick, are attached to shelves with 15-ga. finish nails.

Shelf

5/16 in.

14°

Key shorter than slot depth

DOVETAIL

Shelves, ¾ in. thick by 10 in. wide by 34½ in. long, shoulder to shoulder

⅝ in.

STOPPED DOVETAIL

Bottom shelf, 9¼ in. wide

Apron, ¾ in. thick by 4¼ in. wide by 34½ in. long, is glued to shelf and screwed to sides.

2½ in.

1 in.

Glue block, 1 in. by 1 in. by 3½ in. long

1¾ in.

Glue block adds strength.

Pocket screws

GLUE BLOCK

Shelf Spacing

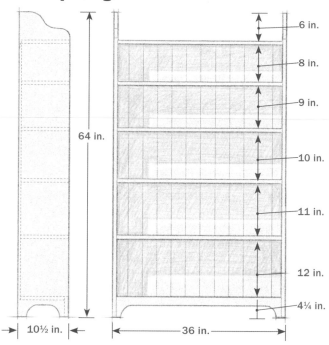

64 in.

6 in.

8 in.

9 in.

10 in.

11 in.

12 in.

4¼ in.

10½ in.

36 in.

corresponding face of the key—makes it easy to slide the shelf in from the back without binding, and creates a wedging action in front as the shelf is tapped home.

The amount of taper is not that critical as long as it is consistent. I keep the taper to about ⅟₃₂ in. (about as thick as three business cards) per 10 in. of board width. With a taper like this, the joint can be almost completely assembled for trial fitting, and can be driven home with a few mallet blows.

Router method simplifies complex joint

Tapered sliding dovetails can be cut by hand, using saws and chisels, but this method can be imprecise and time-consuming. I prefer to use a router and a few simple jigs to do the job. The method is clean and allows you

Attach a cleat to each case side. Screw the plywood cleat to the top of the inside case sides and perfectly square to the edges. Place screws in areas that will be wasted away when you profile the ends.

Clamp the fence to the workpiece. Align the front edge of the fence flush with the back of the case side and tight against the cleat at the top.

Router Setup

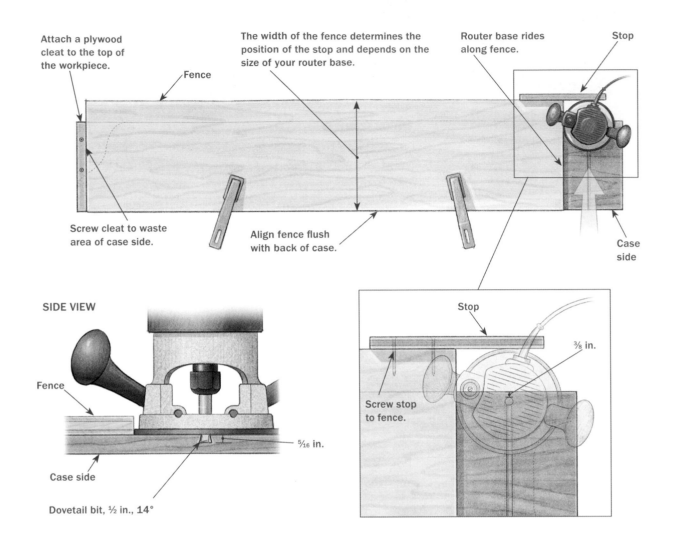

Attach a plywood cleat to the top of the workpiece.

Fence

The width of the fence determines the position of the stop and depends on the size of your router base.

Router base rides along fence.

Stop

Screw cleat to waste area of case side.

Align fence flush with back of case.

Case side

SIDE VIEW

Fence

Case side

Dovetail bit, ½ in., 14°

5/16 in.

Stop

Screw stop to fence.

3/8 in.

to dial in the fit of each joint. To avoid confusion, be sure to label mating parts as you work.

Cut slots with a handheld router

For strength, the slot should be no deeper than half the thickness of the side. Likewise, the thin part of the key should be at least half the thickness of the shelf, and the length at least one-third the thickness of the shelf.

First, screw a ¾-in.-thick plywood cleat to the top of the case sides (see the left photo on p. 55). Mark the shelf locations on each side, then make a ¾-in.-thick plywood fence to locate the slots in both sides. Cut the fence to a length that aligns the router bit with the lower shelf location, and rip it to a width that will place the router bit ⅜ in. from the front of the side. Screw a stop to the business end of the fence, and clamp the assembly in place (see the drawing above).

For the second pass, shim out the back side.
Place the shim between the fence and the cleat.
Veneer tape is the perfect thickness (1/32 in.) to
create the desired taper.

Add a Shim to Create the Taper

Rout the slot. Holding the router tight against the fence for
control, cut until you reach the stop. Let the bit stop spinning
before backing it out of the slot, or you could ruin the cut.

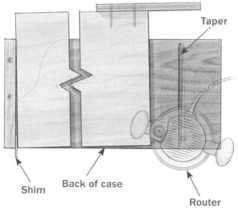

Taper

Shim   Back of case

Router

Set the router to make a 5/16-in.-deep cut
and rout the slot across the side until you
reach the stop. Next, remove the fence and
place a shim between the rear edge of the
cleat and the rear edge of the fence. Reclamp
the fence in place, then pass the router
through the slot to create the taper along the
bottom edge. Repeat this operation in the
opposite side of the case. Once you have both
slots for the bottom shelf routed and tapered,
trim the fence to cut slots for the next higher
shelf and repeat all of the previous steps.

Now is a good time to cut the bracket feet
on the bottom of the sides, as well as the
profile on top. Clean up those edges before
proceeding.

Reclamp and rerout. With the shim in place
and the fence reclamped, run the router through
the slot to add the taper.

Trim the fence. After routing both slots for the bottom shelf, cut the fence down to repeat the process on the next set of slots.

Cut keys on the router table

Place the same bit you used to cut the slots into the router table, and set the depth so that it's a hair less (0.005 in. or so) than the depth of the slots. This will create a tiny gap to make the sliding action easier. Using a test piece the same thickness as the shelves, (see photo at center right) adjust the fence and take light cuts on both sides until the test piece fits about halfway or more into a slot with hand pressure. Once you've reached that point, you are ready to rout the actual shelves.

First, add a shim to the bottom rear of each shelf. The shim should be the same thickness as the shim used to taper the slots. Rout the top side of the key on each end of each shelf. Then flip each shelf to cut the bottom of the keys. At this point, each shelf should slide freely about halfway home but tightly after that. To fit the shelves individually, make hairline passes across the top, straight side of each key until the shelf slides to within 1½ in. of being fully home

Test piece gets you started. Take light passes along both edges of a test piece, made from a shelf offcut, until it slides halfway or more into a slot with hand pressure.

Shim out the bottom rear of the shelves. Use a shim of the same thickness used to taper the slots. Veneer tape is great because you can iron it on and take it off easily.

Taper the Dovetail Keys

Shim the rear edge of the shelf bottom and rout both sides of the shelf end.

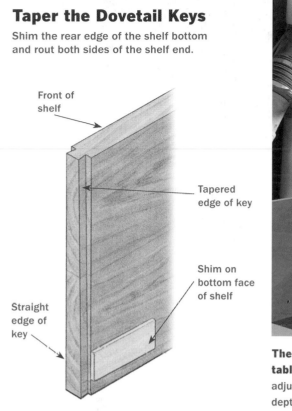

Front of shelf

Tapered edge of key

Shim on bottom face of shelf

Straight edge of key

The keys are cut and tapered at the router table using the same bit that cut the slots, adjusted so that its height is a hair under the slot depth. Use a tall auxiliary fence to keep the long workpieces stable.

Fine-tune the fit. Keep making hairline passes on the router table to get the key to slide closer to home. To micro-adjust the fit, use a sanding block cut to the same angle as the dovetail bit and attach adhesive-backed P120-grit sandpaper to it (above). The goal is to get the shelf to slide with just hand pressure until it is about 1½ in. from being fully home (right).

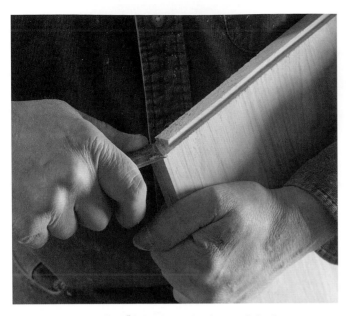

with only hand pressure (see the bottom photos on p. 59). Use a small, angled sanding block to dial in the fit.

Next, use a handsaw and a chisel to trim ⅝ in. from the front of the keys. Refine the fit with the sanding block if needed. Now rout a groove under the top shelf, ¼ in. from the back edge, for the back boards. Next, rip the lower shelves to size along their back edges, and trim an additional ¾ in. off the front of the bottom shelf to accommodate the apron. Finally, cut the rabbets that hold the back boards.

Trim ⅝ in. from the front of the key. Use a handsaw to remove most of the waste, and clean up the cut with a sharp chisel.

Push and pound. Stand the sides rear-edge up on an assembly bench. To install each shelf, place a spot of glue inside the corresponding slots near the front edge. Push in the shelf as far as you can by hand and fist, then rap the shelf home with a mallet.

Nail in the back boards in order. Slide the top edges of the boards into the groove under the top shelf. To avoid misses, mark the shelf locations across the back, then nail each board to each shelf with 15-ga. finish nails.

Glue in shelves, then add back boards

Once you have all the shelves fitted to the sides, the hardest work is done. Now's the time to glue up the case and cut and fit the back boards and apron.

The maple back boards are ripped to random widths no wider than 3½ in. Once the boards are cut to final size, use a raised-panel cove cutter to rout a ¼-in. tongue along their tops. Then rout the rabbets along their sides to create the shiplap.

To glue in the shelves, stand the sides rear-edge up on an assembly bench. Place a spot of glue inside the corresponding slots near the front edge, slide in the shelf as far as you can with hand pressure, then tap the shelf home with a mallet. When installing the bottom shelf, put the apron in place to serve as a stop. Later you can screw the apron into place.

After installing the apron and glue blocks, the piece is ready for finishing (the back boards are finished before final installation). For this bookcase, I sprayed on Deft® clear lacquer.

After you have the back boards in place, the bookcase is ready for your collection of Russian nesting dolls.

Bookcases Transform an Unused Wall

BRENT BENNER

I like books, the kind with paper pages and dust jackets, and I hope they survive the rise in popularity of electronic books. But then, I spend my days building cabinets, not computers. And lucky for me, although e-books might be diminishing the need for bookshelves, there always will be a demand for attractive, efficient storage spaces and quality construction.

This project started when my clients realized that they needed more storage space for books in their Manhattan apartment. The target area was a wall in the bedroom that had two closet doors. The challenge was designing the bookcases around the steel door jambs and between mechanical chases and irregular plaster walls. Because I would build everything in my shop, I had to have accurate site measurements. I figured that making both horizontal and vertical story poles was the best way to avoid mistakes. I marked on the story poles the door locations, plumbing chases, and spaces needed so that I would have room to scribe the bookcases to the walls.

In general, it's a really good idea to measure the walls where a cabinet's face frames will intersect, not back at the corner. (This was especially true here because the walls in this apartment were concrete, out of square, and not parallel.) Back in the shop, I based all my measurements on the pole, which meant there was a lot less chance of a transcription or math error.

Measure On Site

Use a story pole to determine the exact horizontal and vertical size of a space. It's more accurate than using a measuring tape. Take two long pieces of 1x2 and extend them to each side, then mark where they cross. Chases, door frames, and other obstacles can be marked right on the poles. Although it's tempting to measure only at the plane of the wall, it's best also to measure the walls, top and bottom, where the face frames will intersect. Take the poles back to the shop, and use the measurements to build the drawing.

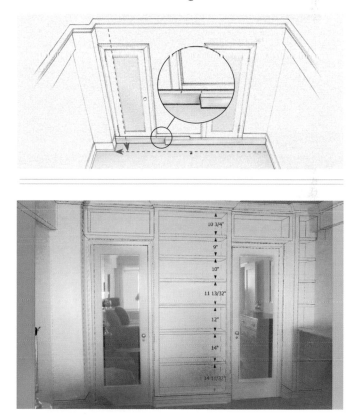

Design on site, virtually. Start a design by taking a photo of the intended space and importing it into Google SketchUp; then scale the drawing over the photo. This helps the client to see what the finished bookcase will look like and ensures that everyone is on the same page before the first piece of wood is cut.

63

Rip, then rabbet. Start by ripping the plywood to width and cutting rabbets for the corners and back with a dado stack. After marking the dado positions for the shelves, use a T-square dado jig to guide a router through the dadoes. Use a $^{23}/_{32}$-in. straight plywood bit so that the shelves fit snugly.

Assemble the box. Glue the rabbeted corners together, and apply bar clamps. To keep the sides from distorting, lay a piece of plywood that's cut to the overall width of the box across the sides to act as a gauge.

Production shelving. After cutting the shelves and nosing to length, biscuit and glue them together. It's faster to clamp them in pairs, using scrap as cauls to spread out the clamping pressure.

Make the frame and attach. Bead the face-frame stock on a router table, and then cut it to length. Miter the beads, then assemble the rails and stiles with pocket screws. After the shelves are glued and tacked into their dadoes, biscuit, glue, and clamp the face frame onto the box.

To visualize the project and solve design issues, after measuring the space I also took a couple of photos of the location and then drafted a design with the help of Google® SketchUp® (see the photo on p. 63). SketchUp has received lots of notice lately as a user-friendly application that makes designing projects easier, especially if you don't have a pricier CAD program (SketchUp is free).

The idea was to use the available space, so I drew a big cabinet between the doors, and a narrow cabinet on one side. A short cabinet would sit above each of the doors and tie the unit together. All told, the cabinets would create about 35 cu. ft. of book space.

Building a strong cabinet is time well spent

Bookcases are simple to build and a great project for woodworkers of all skill levels. I built the cases and shelves with ¾-in. cabinet-grade plywood and the face frames with ¾-in. poplar. To make the boxes stiff and avoid the bother of nailing cleats, I used ½-in. cabinet-grade plywood for the backs. After ripping the box sides to width, I made a story pole to lay out the shelf spacing and then used it to mark the sides. Although I often make adjustable shelves, for this project I used fixed shelves that were fitted into dadoes on the cabinet sides. This arrangement gave the cabinet more rigidity. I glued and clamped the box sides and shelves together, and tacked them with a couple of finish nails per joint. Once the basic box was assembled, I cut the plywood to fit the back, then stapled and glued it into place.

Next, I attached the poplar face frame. To give the project a custom look, I milled the stock to size and then added a bead detail that was mitered at the corners. I joined the face-frame sections together with pocket screws and then fastened the entire frame to the case with glue and biscuits. I also primed and finish-painted everything before installation to save time, although the clients eventually settled on another color.

Make the boxes fit

To support a bookcase, I usually build a separate base from 3-in.-wide strips of ¾-in. plywood that resembles a shipping pallet. Because each base is separate, it can be leveled and aligned prior to positioning

(continued on p. 68)

Separate bases make installation easier. After cutting the existing trim back with a multitool or reciprocating saw, place and level the cabinet bases. Made slightly smaller than the cabinets, the bases can be adjusted so that they're flush to the cabinets' faces while avoiding discrepancies in the corners or intersections of walls and floors. Once shimmed level, they can be screwed to the floor.

Scribe to fit, then set aside. With the cabinet positioned plumb and level, the scribe is set to the amount of overhang on the right. (Benner uses FastCap®'s AccuScribe, but any compass will work.) Follow the contour of the wall, and mark the cabinet's left side. Cut to the line with a jigsaw set to a 15° angle. The back cut makes it easier to make any adjustments to the scribe with a hand plane and/or sandpaper.

Fit the cases in order

The left-hand cabinet (1) was scribed first, the middle cabinet (2) was checked for its fit, and the right-hand cabinet (3) was scribed in place. After the left-hand and middle cabinets were screwed into the wall and to each other, the right-hand cabinet was attached to the wall, and the last cabinet (4) was screwed to the adjacent cabinets.

the bookcases (see the top photo on p. 66). As these tall bookcases extended from the floor to the ceiling, I could also stand them upright and then place them on the base without hitting the ceiling.

Once the bases are in position, I like to start on one side and fit each cabinet, then set it aside (see the bottom three photos on p. 66). After the scribes are complete, I assemble the cabinets (see p. 67). At this job, I started with the short left-hand cabinet. Next, the large middle cabinet had to be fit between two doorways. The thin right-hand cabinet had to be scribed around a horizontal chase and along an unplumb wall. On complicated scribes like this, it's best to remove stock in stages and test the fit as you go, rather than try to scribe and cut all in one pass. The walls were also a problem. Working with conventionally framed stud walls, I screw the cabinets to the framing, hiding the screws if possible. At this job, the walls were concrete, and I used concrete screws that required pilot holes to secure the bookcase. It was easy enough to fasten the baseboard to the cabinet bases, but I had to glue triangular blocking to the ceiling so that I could nail up the crown molding.

The last component of this job was the trim. I had to match the existing profiles, but instead of having a custom profile made, I found an online molding catalog (www. gardenstatelumber.com) and ordered what I needed. I coped the new stock to the old with a coping foot made for a jigsaw. I also made use of my narrow-profile air-powered sander to adjust the fit of the copes. Finally, a shoe molding obscured any discrepancies between the baseboard and the flooring.

Tricks for trim. On this job, the concrete walls and ceiling were somewhat uneven, and the crown would need plenty of nailing to make it conform to the ceiling and to match the existing crown. I glued triangular blocks with construction adhesive so that there would be backing on 16-in. centers. The crown was installed left to right, the bottom reveal was kept constant, and the top of the profile was adjusted as needed.

Make final adjustments. After I roughed out the basic cope with a miter saw and a jigsaw, I used an air-powered narrow-profile sander to fine-tune the cut.

The baseboard was also installed left to right. To make tight miter joints, I cut both halves of the outside miter a little long and pinned them together before scribing them into their final positions. A shoe molding covers any discrepancies between the floor and the baseboard.

Sleek Console Built for Today's TVs

ANATOLE BURKIN

I was the last man on my block, maybe in the entire country, to buy a wide-screen digital television. Like many people, I used to hide my television in an entertainment armoire, but the latest flat-screen televisions have a modern look that I find attractive. Also, it takes a pretty huge cabinet to contain them. So instead of hiding the TV, I hung it on the wall and decided to build a sleek entertainment credenza to go under it.

Made of ¾-in.-thick sapele plywood and solid sapele and wenge, the piece fits into the modernist style—with its clean, crisp lines, no exposed joinery, and no frame-and-panel doors, just long expanses of beautiful sapele grain framed by darker wenge.

Style, however, does not trump function. This credenza offers plenty of storage. Inside are three compartments hidden by three sliding doors. The center section holds the electronics: DVD player, receiver, cable box, and a laptop. The outer sections have banks of drawers to store CDs, DVDs, and other accessories, like headphones and cables. If you don't own a lot of CDs and DVDs, you could easily eliminate the drawers and use that space to hold game consoles or other electronic gear or even change the overall dimensions. The design is quite versatile.

Start with the carcase joinery

Rough-cut the plywood to manageable pieces using a circular saw and an edge guide. Make the final cuts using the tablesaw and a sled. You'll need to cut the top and bottom ½ in. longer than shown in the drawing on pp. 72–73. I did this to make the joinery simpler to cut. These two pieces will be trimmed ¼ in. on each end after cutting the mortises. Use a block plane to clean up any sawmarks on the edges.

(continued on p. 75)

Super-Strong Corner Joint for Plywood

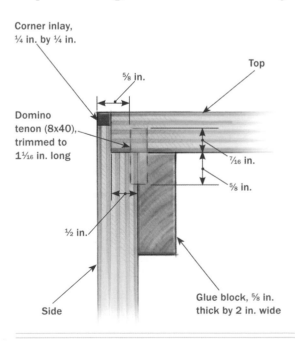

Corner inlay, ¼ in. by ¼ in.

⅝ in.

Top

Domino tenon (8x40), trimmed to 1¹⁄₁₆ in. long

⁷⁄₁₆ in.

⅝ in.

½ in.

Side

Glue block, ⅝ in. thick by 2 in. wide

Modern Credenza, Modern Construction

The joinery for this modern entertainment credenza was assembled using a modern tool: Festool's Domino machine. But you can easily adapt the design for router-cut mortises and make your own slip tenons.

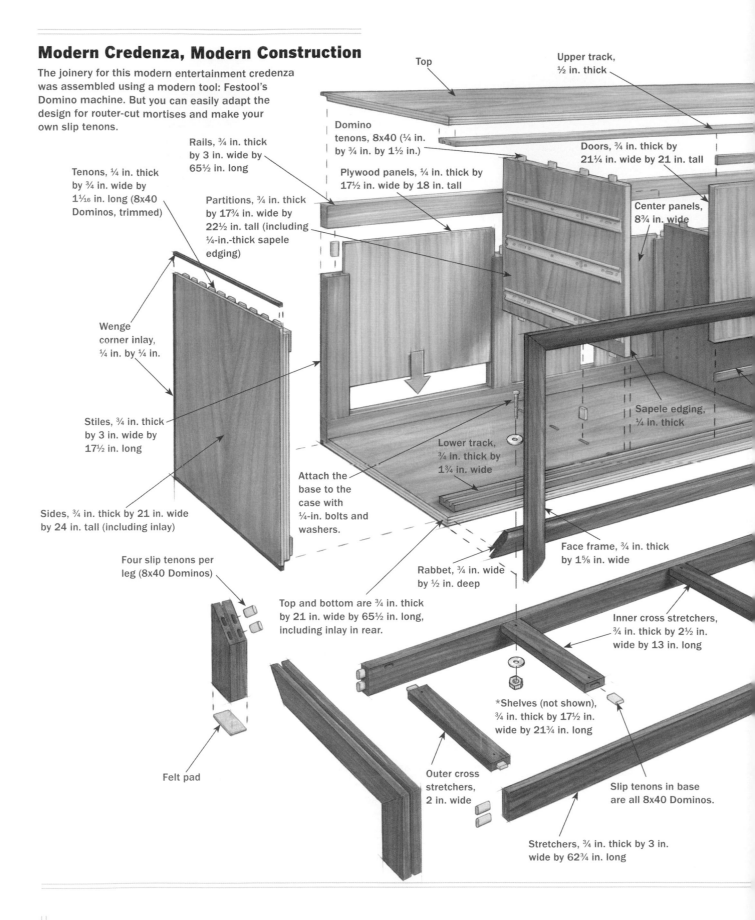

Top

Upper track, ½ in. thick

Domino tenons, 8x40 (¼ in. by ¾ in. by 1½ in.)

Doors, ¾ in. thick by 21¼ in. wide by 21 in. tall

Rails, ¾ in. thick by 3 in. wide by 65½ in. long

Plywood panels, ¼ in. thick by 17½ in. wide by 18 in. tall

Center panels, 8¾ in. wide

Tenons, ¼ in. thick by ¾ in. wide by 1¹⁄₁₆ in. long (8x40 Dominos, trimmed)

Partitions, ¾ in. thick by 17¾ in. wide by 22½ in. tall (including ¼-in.-thick sapele edging)

Wenge corner inlay, ¼ in. by ¼ in.

Sapele edging, ¼ in. thick

Stiles, ¾ in. thick by 3 in. wide by 17½ in. long

Lower track, ¾ in. thick by 1¾ in. wide

Attach the base to the case with ¼-in. bolts and washers.

Sides, ¾ in. thick by 21 in. wide by 24 in. tall (including inlay)

Face frame, ¾ in. thick by 1⅝ in. wide

Four slip tenons per leg (8x40 Dominos)

Rabbet, ¾ in. wide by ½ in. deep

Top and bottom are ¾ in. thick by 21 in. wide by 65½ in. long, including inlay in rear.

Inner cross stretchers, ¾ in. thick by 2½ in. wide by 13 in. long

*Shelves (not shown), ¾ in. thick by 17½ in. wide by 21¾ in. long

Felt pad

Outer cross stretchers, 2 in. wide

Slip tenons in base are all 8x40 Dominos.

Stretchers, ¾ in. thick by 3 in. wide by 62¾ in. long

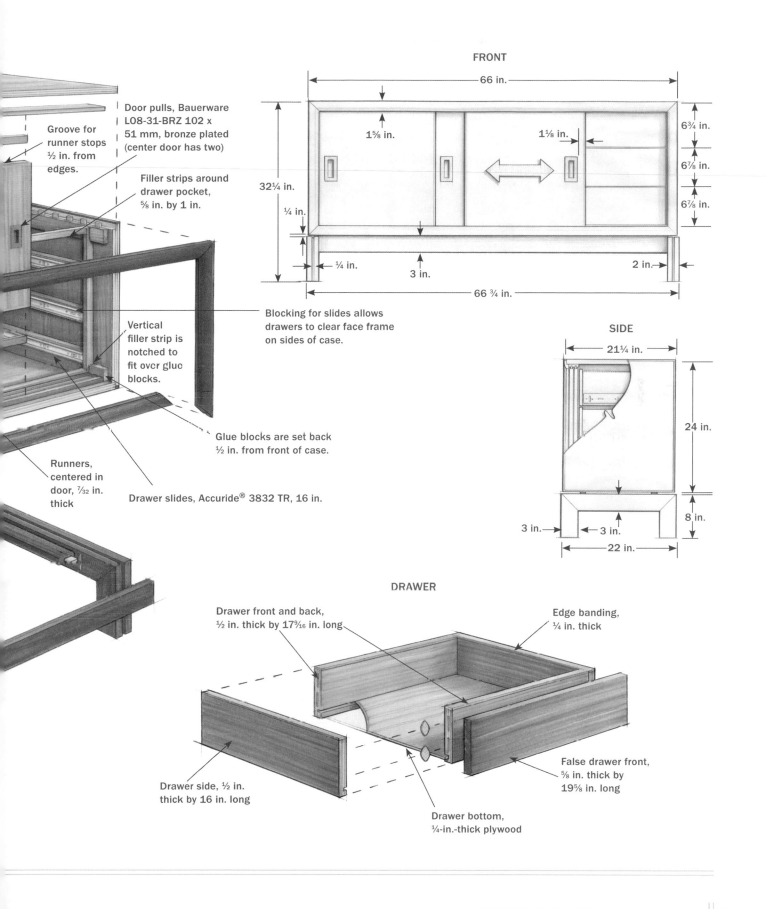

FRONT

66 in.

1⅝ in.

1⅛ in.

32¼ in.

¼ in.

¼ in.

3 in.

66 ¾ in.

6¾ in.

6⅞ in.

6⅞ in.

2 in.

Groove for
runner stops
½ in. from
edges.

Door pulls, Bauerware
LO8-31-BRZ 102 x
51 mm, bronze plated
(center door has two)

Filler strips around
drawer pocket,
⅝ in. by 1 in.

Vertical
filler strip is
notched to
fit over glue
blocks.

Runners,
centered in
door, 7⁄32 in.
thick

Blocking for slides allows
drawers to clear face frame
on sides of case.

Glue blocks are set back
½ in. from front of case.

Drawer slides, Accuride® 3832 TR, 16 in.

SIDE

21¼ in.

24 in.

8 in.

3 in.

3 in.

22 in.

DRAWER

Drawer front and back,
½ in. thick by 17⁹⁄₁₆ in. long

Edge banding,
¼ in. thick

Drawer side, ½ in.
thick by 16 in. long

False drawer front,
⅝ in. thick by
19⅝ in. long

Drawer bottom,
¼-in.-thick plywood

Glue blocks beef up the corners. The glue blocks, attached to the top and bottom of each side, increase strength against racking.

More tenons, more strength. Festool's Domino creates rows of slip-tenon joints in minutes. In the sides, the author moved the mortises partway into the glue blocks to accommodate the rabbet that follows.

Use a dado set to rabbet the sides. Bury the blade in a sacrificial fence to dial in the width. Place an offcut from the glue-block stock under the workpiece to stabilize it.

Trim the top. After cutting the mortises in the top and bottom, trim those parts to fit inside the rabbets in the sides.

Next, use a dado set to rabbet the back of all four carcase parts. Glue blocks on the inside corners strengthen the case and provide a stable platform when routing the mortises in the sides. Mill up the blocks and glue them flush to the top and bottom edges, and ½ in. back from the front edge to allow for the face frame.

Cut mortises for the slip tenons

A fence-equipped router works fine to cut the mortises for this project, but I splurged last year and bought a Festool® Domino® joiner, which makes really fast work of mortise-and-tenon joinery. The tool cuts a deep mortise in one plunge, like a biscuit joiner. I used the Domino's medium-thickness bit and tenons, set to cut as deeply as possible into the sides, but just shy of blowing through the top and bottom panels.

No matter what tool you use, mark out the joinery using a story stick. Once that's done, go ahead and start cutting mortises. Use the outside faces of the carcase components as reference points for the fence of your router or Domino.

I put ¼-in. wenge inlay in each corner of this plywood case, which not only adds a nice contrast but also offers a more durable edge. The rabbet joints are designed to leave a pocket for this inlay.

Rabbet the top and bottom of the sides using a dado set, sneaking up on a good fit. You will have removed some of the mortise depth, hence the deep initial cuts. Next, trim ¼ in. off each end of the top and bottom to accommodate the rabbets.

Finally, cut the partitions to size and drill the shelf-pin holes in them for the adjustable shelves. Add the solid-wood edging on the front, and cut the mortises in the partitions and the top and bottom for the slip tenons.

Dry-fit and glue up the case

When it comes to gluing up the case, a dry run is critical. It gives you a chance to rehearse the steps, check the joints, and be sure you have enough clamps at the ready. Because the rabbets effectively reduce the depth of the mortises on the sides, stock Domino tenons have to be trimmed.

Cut the partition joinery.
To align the mortises in the top and bottom, use a spacer board to guide the Domino joiner. Reference the spacer board off the side, which should be dry-fitted in place.

Get the glue on. Begin by gluing the slip tenons to the vertical members. Then apply glue to the mortises of the top and bottom. Clamp along the edges and use cauls to bring home the partitions.

Glue the tenons into the sides and partitions, then fit them to the top and bottom. Assemble the case, making sure to check for square. For the inlay along the top, bottom, and back, mill up strips of wenge just a hair over ¼ in. square and glue them in; I used a pin nailer instead of clamps to hold the pieces in place. The pins are set deep enough to be out of the way later when I plane the inlay flush.

Add the back

The back assembly is a solid-wood sapele frame with ¼-in.-thick sapele-faced MDF (or plywood) panels. The end panels are fixed; the center panels are removable for easy access to wiring.

Plane the frame assembly to fit the carcase, then screw it in place. I didn't glue the frame, figuring that in a few years I might want to change the inside of the case due to technology updates.

Fill the rabbets. Glue and nail (or tape) the wenge inlay strips to the corners and back edges of the case. Trim them flush after the glue dries.

Glued-in panels create a rigid assembly. A sturdy back helps strengthen the case against racking. The two outer panels are glued into their grooves (right); the two center panels (not shown) are removable. The frame is connected with slip tenons and screwed into the cabinet (below).

Attach the front face frame

A solid wenge face frame decorates the front of the case. The frame is mitered and rabbeted to fit over the plywood. I also shaped the front face with a massive roundover bit (2¹⁹/₃₂ in., Freud® No. 99-027) to soften the look of this otherwise squarish credenza.

Mill up the frame pieces, rabbet them, miter the corners, then glue them in place. Again, a pin nailer comes in handy.

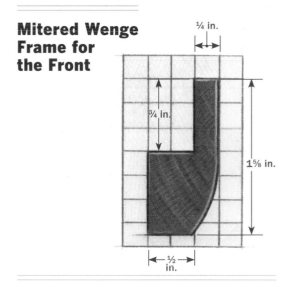

Mitered Wenge Frame for the Front

¼ in.

¾ in.

1⅝ in.

½ in.

Roundover on the router table. Rout the profile of the front face frame on the stock before cutting the miters. Fair the shape with handplanes, scrapers, and sandpaper.

Sled makes better miters. After rabbeting the back of the face frame stock, cut the miters using a sled. Place a scrap piece in the rabbet to support the workpiece.

Glue the frame to the front. Rather than fussing with clamps, Burkin used pins to hold the pieces in place. Pieces are cut, fit, and nailed one at a time.

Tackle the doors, drawers, and shelves

The sliding doors are ¾-in. plywood edged with solid sapele. Cut the plywood to size and apply the edging. The corners of the doors will be mostly hidden, so don't bother mitering the edging. Cut stopped grooves in the top and bottom edges using a slot-cutting bit in a router table. Insert runners or guides of resawn solid sapele, but don't glue them yet.

Make the tracks from solid stock. Note that the top track is thinner than the lower track (see the drawing at right). Cut the grooves on the tablesaw, making them a hair

Smooth Sliding Door

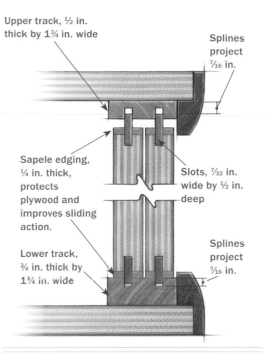

Upper track, ½ in. thick by 1¾ in. wide

Splines project ⁷⁄₁₆ in.

Sapele edging, ¼ in. thick, protects plywood and improves sliding action.

Slots, ⁷⁄₃₂ in. wide by ½ in. deep

Lower track, ¾ in. thick by 1¾ in. wide

Splines project ³⁄₁₆ in.

Make tracks. The top track is thinner than the lower track. After cutting the grooves on the tablesaw, screw the tracks inside the case.

Install the runners. Rout stopped grooves in the top and bottom of the doors. Dry-fit the runners, then check the fit and action of the doors. You may have to adjust the height of the runners to get them to fit nicely.

Lift and drop. The doors are inserted from the front by tipping them into the center bay (without shelves in place). Lift the door to engage the top track first, then drop it into the lower track.

wider than the guides for smooth operation. Screw the tracks in place.

The doors are inserted from the front by tipping them into the center bay (without shelves in place), then lifting them to engage the top track first, and dropping them into the lower track (see the bottom right photo on p. 79). You may have to adjust the height of the splines to get the doors to fit.

There should be a slight gap, ¹⁄₁₆ in. or so, between the front and rear doors, as well as the face frame. Once you have the doors fitted to your liking, glue the guides into the doors.

I used bronze-finished metal pulls because I like a bit of metal on a modern piece. After excavating the mortises for the pulls, I used epoxy to bond the metal to the wood.

To continue the clean look inside, the drawers have no pulls. Instead, I chose full-extension touch-release slides that pop out

Tenons brace the corners. Each miter gets four slip tenons.

Glue up the mitered feet first (above), then attach them to the stretcher assembly (right).

Bolt the base to the case. Drill clearance holes through the base and bottom of the case, then bolt the assembly in place.

the drawer when you push on the front. The slides provide smooth action and full access to the drawer. The drawers are ½-in. sapele plywood edged with solid sapele, with solid sapele false fronts. Shelves are ¾-in.-thick sapele plywood edged with solid wenge on the front.

Solid-wood base can handle the load

The case sits on solid wenge legs joined with stretchers, all laminated for extra thickness (I could find only 4/4 stock locally). The legs are slightly proud of the case on the front, sides, and rear, and the stretchers are inset to give the illusion that the case is floating. To add a shadow line, the center lamination is

¼ in. narrower than the outside pieces. It is glued flush to one side, and indented ¼ in. on the show face. Plane and sand the show edge before glue-up, because it won't be easy to do later.

Building the base is straightforward. The corners are mitered and joined with quadruple slip tenons. A pair of stretchers ¼-in. proud of the top of the legs join the leg assemblies. Four short cross-stretchers provide support and attachment points for the case.

For the finish, a Danish Modern look goes well, nothing too glossy or grain filling. Good choices are wipe-on finishes such as Minwax Poly or Waterlox®. Wax the door bottoms and guides for smooth action.

A Low Console for a Home Theater

STEVE CASEY

Just a few years ago, building an entertainment center for a large-screen TV meant designing a case piece big enough to hide an elephant. Today's slimmer sets can hang on a wall or sit attractively in the open, offering furniture makers new options. Among the most practical is a low console that can house media and electronics. It's a great way to bring that glorious high-definition picture out of the armoire.

I designed this console for a self-contained small home-theater system built around a 52-in. projection-style TV, but it would work just as well with a slimmer flat-panel model. Visually, it's tasteful and tame enough to harmonize with quite a few furniture styles, and you can feel free to adapt its style to fit your room. Look below the surface, though, and it becomes clear this piece is media furniture through and through.

At 24 in. tall, the console is still low enough to place the center of most TVs at eye level for a seated viewer. And it's strong enough to support any set, so you won't need a tricky wall-mount.

At 22 in. deep, the cabinet will comfortably hold most electronic components. I designed the drawers specifically to house DVDs and CDs without making the case too tall. The back and shelves are engineered to promote ventilation for the equipment and to simplify cable management. And I put the whole piece on casters so it would be easy to pull away from the wall for system setup, maintenance, or cleaning. Small casters will work on a hardwood floor, but carpet calls for larger ones.

None of those features call attention to themselves. What you see and live with is a nice piece of furniture. The project is a

(continued on p. 85)

Media-Friendly Features

A back that breathes. Multiple cutouts provide ample airflow for electronic components. The recessed back also creates space behind the piece for cords to drop freely.

Tall drawers. Side-mounted slides allow deep storage for DVDs, and CDs. Dividers keep everything organized.

Open shelving. The components are accessible to hands and remote controls and become part of the design. The center shelving adjusts to fit a wide variety of components.

Hidden wheels. Six casters make it easy to reach the back for setup, maintenance, or cleaning. The wheels are inset to avoid a distracting gap between the floor and the bottom of the piece.

good example of building a sturdy carcase in an efficient way, using sheet goods and techniques I developed and use for building large-scale entertainment center furniture and cabinetry.

Sheet goods make a stable case

One of the greatest challenges in building furniture to house electronic equipment is that the gear generates heat that causes wood movement. So, I always use stable composite material (in this case, two sheets of cherry plywood) for media furniture carcases.

The first step is to lay out and cut the carcase parts. When cutting sheet goods, never assume that the original edges are straight or square. If you want a 20-in.-wide finished piece, cut it at least ⅛ in. larger, then turn it around and cut off the factory edge. If things are not square, it is usually best to square the ends of smaller ripped parts rather than the whole sheet. After all the parts are cut, I drill holes for adjustable shelves in the equipment rack space. Then I join the carcase together.

The carcase is joined entirely with biscuits and screws—no dadoes, no rabbets, no

The fixed shelves are first. Construction begins with two H-shaped subassemblies (above). These assemblies are then connected by a plywood bottom (left). The space between them creates the central shelving area.

Solid-wood stretchers connect the piece at the top. These also create a place to attach the back and top of the cabinet. The front stretcher protrudes ¾ in. from the case, to meet the other edging, so Casey uses a piece of ¾-in. scrap to set the reveal.

Efficient Construction

The plywood carcase is held together with biscuits and screws. Solid-wood drawer faces, end caps, and edging give the piece a furniture feel.

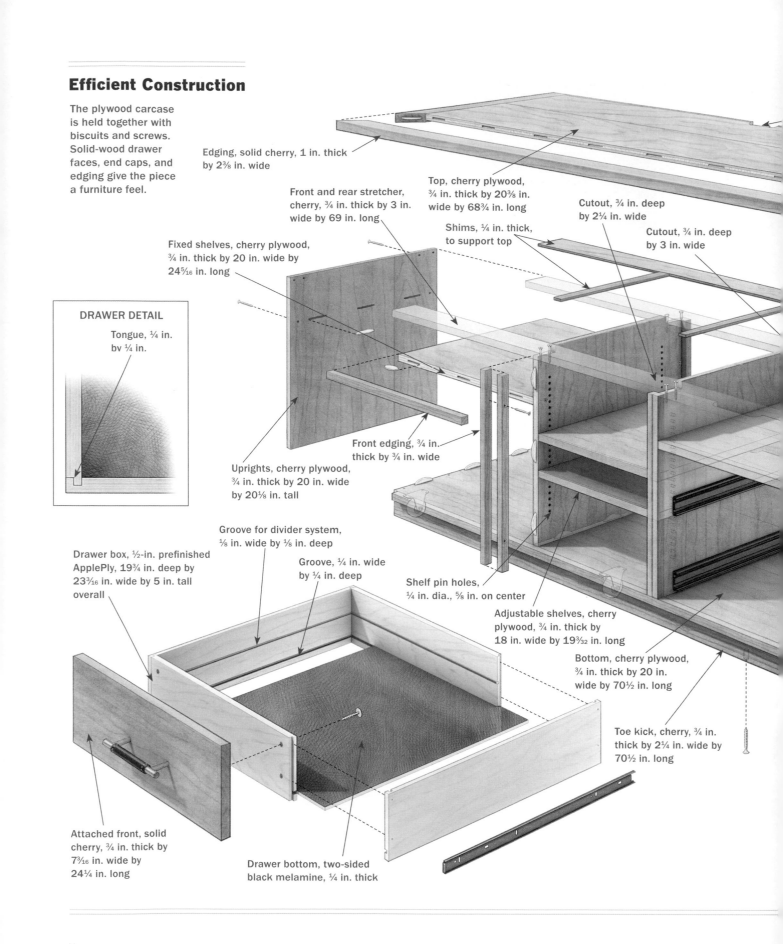

Edging, solid cherry, 1 in. thick by 2⅜ in. wide

Top, cherry plywood, ¾ in. thick by 20⅜ in. wide by 68¾ in. long

Front and rear stretcher, cherry, ¾ in. thick by 3 in. wide by 69 in. long

Cutout, ¾ in. deep by 2¼ in. wide

Cutout, ¾ in. deep by 3 in. wide

Fixed shelves, cherry plywood, ¾ in. thick by 20 in. wide by 24⁵⁄₁₆ in. long

Shims, ¼ in. thick, to support top

DRAWER DETAIL

Tongue, ¼ in. by ¼ in.

Front edging, ¾ in. thick by ¾ in. wide

Uprights, cherry plywood, ¾ in. thick by 20 in. wide by 20⅛ in. tall

Groove for divider system, ⅛ in. wide by ⅛ in. deep

Groove, ¼ in. wide by ¼ in. deep

Shelf pin holes, ¼ in. dia., ⅝ in. on center

Drawer box, ½-in. prefinished ApplePly, 19¾ in. deep by 23³⁄₁₆ in. wide by 5 in. tall overall

Adjustable shelves, cherry plywood, ¾ in. thick by 18 in. wide by 19³⁄₃₂ in. long

Bottom, cherry plywood, ¾ in. thick by 20 in. wide by 70½ in. long

Attached front, solid cherry, ¾ in. thick by 7³⁄₁₆ in. wide by 24¼ in. long

Drawer bottom, two-sided black melamine, ¼ in. thick

Toe kick, cherry, ¾ in. thick by 2¼ in. wide by 70½ in. long

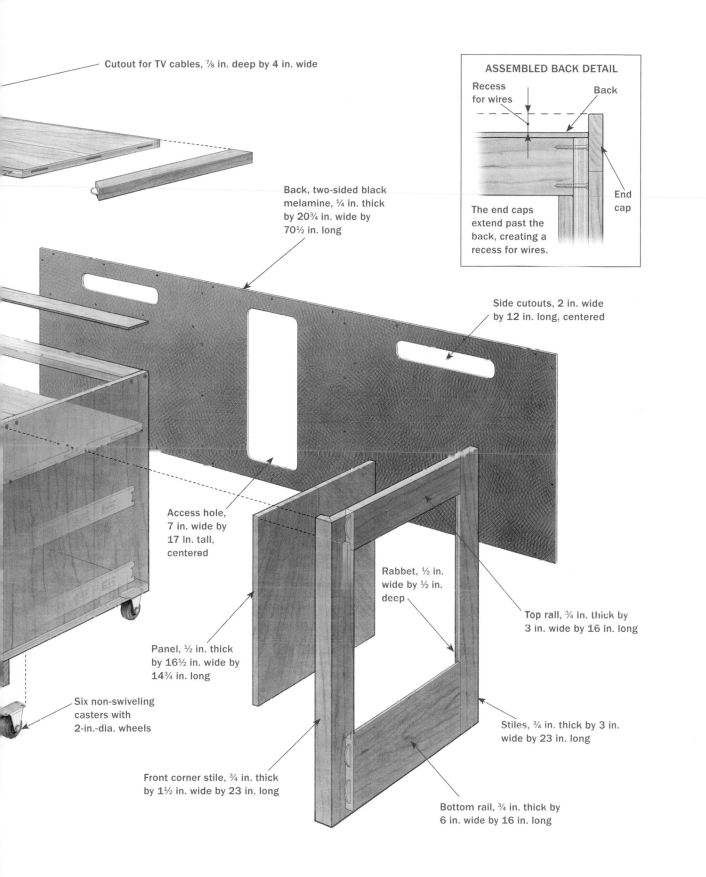

Cutout for TV cables, ⅞ in. deep by 4 in. wide

Back, two-sided black melamine, ¼ in. thick by 20¾ in. wide by 70½ in. long

Side cutouts, 2 in. wide by 12 in. long, centered

Access hole, 7 in. wide by 17 in. tall, centered

Rabbet, ½ in. wide by ½ in. deep

Top rail, ¾ in. thick by 3 in. wide by 16 in. long

Panel, ½ in. thick by 16½ in. wide by 14¾ in. long

Six non-swiveling casters with 2-in.-dia. wheels

Stiles, ¾ in. thick by 3 in. wide by 23 in. long

Front corner stile, ¾ in. thick by 1½ in. wide by 23 in. long

Bottom rail, ¾ in. thick by 6 in. wide by 16 in. long

ASSEMBLED BACK DETAIL

Recess for wires

Back

End cap

The end caps extend past the back, creating a recess for wires.

glue. I don't want to chip out the veneer on a new sheet of plywood while cutting dado and rabbet joinery, or fret over squeeze-out marring my finish in the corners. A glueless carcase also lets me disassemble the piece as needed during construction to check fit and measurements, making it much easier to fix mistakes.

There's no harm, of course, in using glue if you want to. But, after years of gluing everything to last an eternity, I've discovered that biscuits and screws are more than strong enough to hold a piece like this together ... forever.

I predrill for the screws using a tapered bit with an integral countersink. I use #7, 1⅝-in. bugle-head construction screws with sharp, coarse threads and put them in carefully so they don't strip. It's easy to get splitting near the outside joint edges, so I put a clamp on the thread side of the joint so the wedge action of the screw doesn't split the panel.

The panel for the end cap sits in a rabbet.
Rout the rabbet with a bearing-guided bit and square up the corners with a chisel.

A no-clamp glue-up

Bevel the front stile after glue-up (1). Cutting it beforehand would deprive you of a square clamping surface. The mating piece is cut from the same stock. Strips of painter's tape align the edges and create a hinge for the glue-up (2). Casey wraps the assembly with several bands of painter's tape to secure the pieces (3). No biscuits or clamps are needed.

The mitered return hides the plywood. The panel is prefinished to prevent wood movement from exposing any unfinished areas at the edges.

Attach the solid trim

Solid-wood edging and other details elevate the console's appearance from cabinetry to furniture. The most prominent of these features are the frame-and-panel caps on the ends. The front stiles are cut from the same stock as the side panels and are mitered to wrap the grain continuously from the sides to the face to give it the look of solid stock. The frames are assembled with biscuits, and the inside of each frame is rabbeted to accept a floating panel of ½-in. solid cherry or cherry plywood (see the top photo on the facing page). This creates a ¼-in. reveal for the panel while maintaining consistent thickness for the exterior trim. The assembly is attached with screws driven into the frame from inside the case.

A solid-cherry stretcher across the top of the case combines with solid edging to dress out the rest of the case front (see the bottom photo on p. 85). Before attaching the edging, I hand-sand a small ¹⁄₁₆-in. roundover radius on the inside corners of each adjoining piece of plywood and solid stock, including the pieces on the top. This creates a very fine parting line where the plywood and edging meet, accentuating what many folks would try to hide and, in the process, making an eye-pleasing detail. After the edging is attached, I rout a ³⁄₁₆-in. roundover onto all the outside and inside corners.

The drawers have simple joinery and false fronts

I build the drawers from ½-in.-thick prefinished ApplePly or Europly®. The bottoms are two-sided, ¼-in. black melamine, in keeping with the high-tech contents. The joints are rabbeted, glued, and pinned with brads to hold them together while the glue dries.

I hang the drawers on black, side-mounted, full-extension slides (see the photos on p. 90).

No measuring, no marking. The lower slides sit right on the case bottom. To ensure proper spacing between the slides, the author rips a piece of ½-in. MDF to match the drawer-face height.

Use the spacer to locate the upper slides. With the spacer positioned on top of the lower slide, its top edge supports the upper slide at the correct height for installation.

Attach the matching hardware. Use a combination square referenced off the bottom of the drawer side to pencil a layout line for the runner (left). Mounting screws are centered on this line and driven through factory-drilled holes in the hardware (right).

Undermount slides might yield a cleaner look, but they steal depth from the drawer at the bottom. In a console with limited overall height, this can make the difference between a drawer that can be used for media storage and one that isn't deep enough.

I size the drawer boxes to accommodate a ¾-in.-thick separate front, with the faces recessed very slightly behind the front radius detail. Separate drawer fronts allow for perfect alignment after the piece is finally placed and loaded with equipment.

False fronts and media storage. The author drills oversize holes and uses a 1-in. washerhead screw with a ½-in.-dia head (some manufacturers call them "drawer-front adjusting screws"). This creates wiggle room for slight adjustments in the position of the drawer front to get it square and even in the opening. The central horizontal groove houses the divider hardware.

Edge the top and attach it

The top is plywood with a 1-in. by 2½-in. solid border, which is biscuited and mitered. This three-sided border creates a nice effect, making the piece appear to belong up against a wall. The raw edge on the back of the top is dressed with ¼-in. solid stock.

To make room for the cables that connect the TV to the other equipment, make a small cutout in the back of the top. This also lets some heat escape when the case is tight against the wall. The top is held in place with screws driven from the underside through the solid cross-members of the case. Because the solid border is thicker than the top, you'll need to shim and fill the space between the plywood and the cabinet.

The back is two-sided, ¼-in. black melamine. Although thin, this material creates a rigid back that lends the piece much of its structural strength, so be sure to size the back to fit snugly between the rear stiles of the end caps. I fasten the back with screws countersunk and driven every 8 in. into the rear edges of the plywood carcase.

Get the popcorn ready

Before finishing, break down all removable components, then sand everything that wasn't sanded prior to assembly. I used clear oil to bring up the color before spraying on a standard lacquer finish: one coat of sanding sealer and two coats of 40-sheen lacquer, sanding with 320-grit paper between coats. For an alternative hand-applied topcoat, try dewaxed shellac or a traditional oil finish.

Install the equipment, roll the finished unit into place, and you're all done. Time to pop in a DVD or watch some drivel on TV!

Straight-Ahead Corner Hutch

GARY STRIEGLER

A built-in corner hutch takes beautiful advantage of unused space. Its diagonal layout softens the feel of a room while adding architectural interest. I like this hutch because its finished appearance doesn't betray the fact that it's easy and affordable to build. The carcase, face frame, and shelves are made from ¾-in. medium-density fiberboard (MDF), and the trim details can be created with stock profiles.

The hutch's scale should match the room's scale. For dining rooms, I've found that 42 in. across the face frame provides good shelf depth while maintaining a manageable size that won't intrude on the room. For trim details, I use a selection of stock profiles that give the hutch a classic feel: crown molding, reeded pilasters on plinth blocks, and panel molding all simply applied to the face frame.

The one-piece face frame is the biggest time-saver in this project. This detail eliminates the work needed to assemble the frame from separate stiles and rails.

A template quickly establishes the dimensions

To make a template, I use a 5-in.-wide scrap of plywood or MDF (see the drawing on p. 94). The template gives me the exact location of the hutch, which enables me to measure the width of the carcase sides. The template is 42 in. long, with 45° miters at both ends. A line ¾ in. back from the template's front edge represents the thickness of the face frame.

Hutch Plan

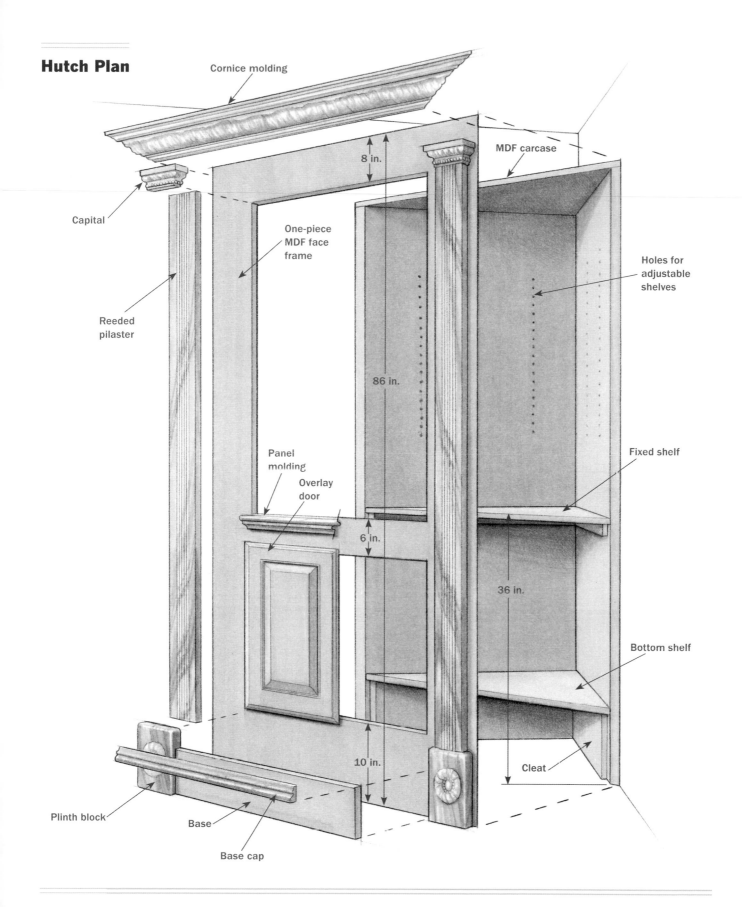

Cornice molding

Capital

Reeded
pilaster

One-piece
MDF face
frame

MDF carcase

Holes for
adjustable
shelves

8 in.

86 in.

Panel
molding

Overlay
door

Fixed shelf

6 in.

36 in.

Bottom shelf

10 in.

Cleat

Plinth block

Base

Base cap

Layout Template

For just-right measurements, use a template.

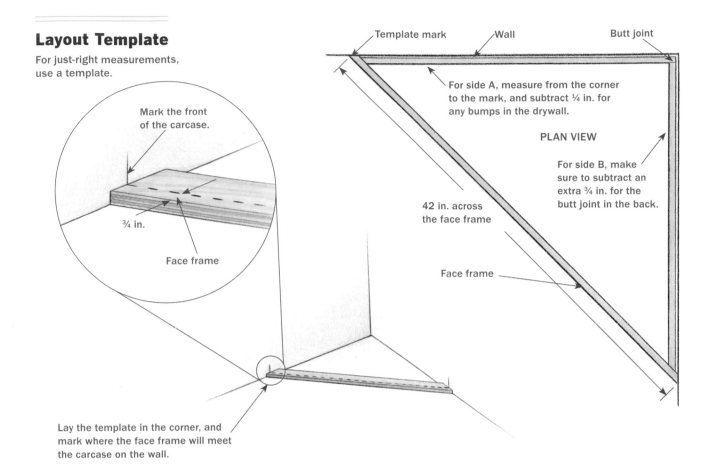

Template mark
Wall
Butt joint

Mark the front of the carcase.

¾ in.

Face frame

For side A, measure from the corner to the mark, and subtract ¼ in. for any bumps in the drywall.

PLAN VIEW

For side B, make sure to subtract an extra ¾ in. for the butt joint in the back.

42 in. across the face frame

Face frame

Lay the template in the corner, and mark where the face frame will meet the carcase on the wall.

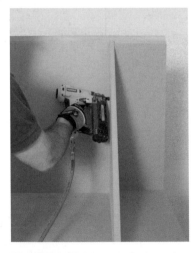

Cut the sides. Tilt the saw base to a 45° bevel and rip the sides, guiding the circular saw against a straight length of MDF.

The fixed shelves are fastened to MDF cleats. To join the sides, use a simple butt joint screwed from the back.

When the carcase is done, plumb and shim it between the layout marks on the wall.

Cut the openings in the face frame with a circular saw. The author uses a plunge cut guided by a straightedge (left). In the corners, he finishes the cut with a handsaw or a jigsaw (above).

Carcase goes together quickly

The two sides are held together by two triangular shelves and a top. The shelves are fastened to cleats, and the top is glued and screwed to the sides from above. The hutch is attached to the framing with a 3-in. screw in each wall near the top of the carcase.

Single-piece face frame requires no joinery

You can save time and money by cutting the face frame from a single piece of MDF. MDF is stable and sturdy, and it takes paint well. I used an 8-in. border on the sides of the face frame. Anything smaller starts to compromise the strength, and anything larger looks clunky and awkward.

The sides of the face frame are cut at a 47° bevel. This makes for a snug fit against the wall and the front of the carcase.

Final touches define the look

Stock trim details give this hutch a classic look. I used crown, capitals, plinths, pilasters, and panel molding from White River Hardwoods-Woodworks, Inc.® (www. mouldings.com). I softened the corner by adding a 5-in.-wide panel in the back and refined the look with a simple beaded molding around the upper opening (see left photo on p. 97). Your local door and window supplier should have a good selection of trim profiles. Online, you can find a nearly limitless variety of embossed and shaped trim profiles. You can build the doors yourself, or you can order them from online suppliers (scherrs.com; lakesidemoulding.com). Just remember that the trim, the door design, and the style of the room all should work together to create a unified look.

To bore holes for shelf-support pins, Striegler uses a self-centering bit and a drilling jig from Rockler Woodworking and Hardware® (rockler.com).

The face frame tilts into place. Make the bottom shelf flush with the face frame, then attach it to the case with 15-ga. finish nails.

Buy or build the doors. The author took the MDF door blanks for this hutch to a local cabinet shop, where a CNC machine milled the profiles.

TIP Compared to edge-mount cup hinges, face-mount, overlay-style cup hinges provide a stronger connection and a cleaner look. The Blum® hinge shown here is from Woodcraft® (#02R80; woodcraft.com).

Store-bought moldings dress up a hutch but keep installation simple.

Beautify Your Home with a Shaker Built-In

CHRISTIAN BECKSVOORT

As a furniture-maker for 30-plus years, I've grown used to the pleasure of working solid wood at the workbench, so it takes some persuasion to get me to leave the shop, haul sheets of plywood, and get on my knees to scribe along crooked walls. But in my younger days, I built my fair share of kitchen cabinets, commercial fixtures, and built-ins. And recently, my most discerning client, my wife, convinced me that we needed a built-in. So out of the shop I went.

Early homes tended to lack closets and storage space, so wardrobes and built-ins were common. The Shakers added built-ins wherever possible and turned them into an art form. Most, if not all, the built-ins made by the Shakers were constructed in place. I did the same, except I used plywood partitions and shelves where the Shakers used solid pine (or poplar in the South). I used solid cherry for the face frames, doors, and drawers.

The best part of a built-in is its versatility. You can design it to function for your particular situation. Mine has a middle bottom section for drawers. The right bottom section has a closet rod, while the left bottom section has adjustable shelves. In our case, the location was under a roof and knee wall next to a doorway. A lot of homes have areas where a slanted ceiling makes the space unsuitable for almost anything else. I started with a rough sketch, consisting of three sections of doors and drawers that would be built in place into a single unit. This built-in navigates the knee wall, but the techniques and order of operations are exactly the same as for a straight built-in. The keys to success are keeping everything plumb and level and having a lot of patience while you go back and forth between the site and the shop.

(continued on p. 102)

TIP To correct for wavy walls or crooked floors, make quick and easy frames out of cheap 1x3 furring strips. Shim behind or under the frames to create flat, level, and plumb surfaces for the built-in.

Anatomy of a Shaker Built-In

Plywood partitions are easy to cut to size and quick to install. Solid-wood face frame pieces are scribed to the wall and ceiling, and then dry-fit to mark their joinery.

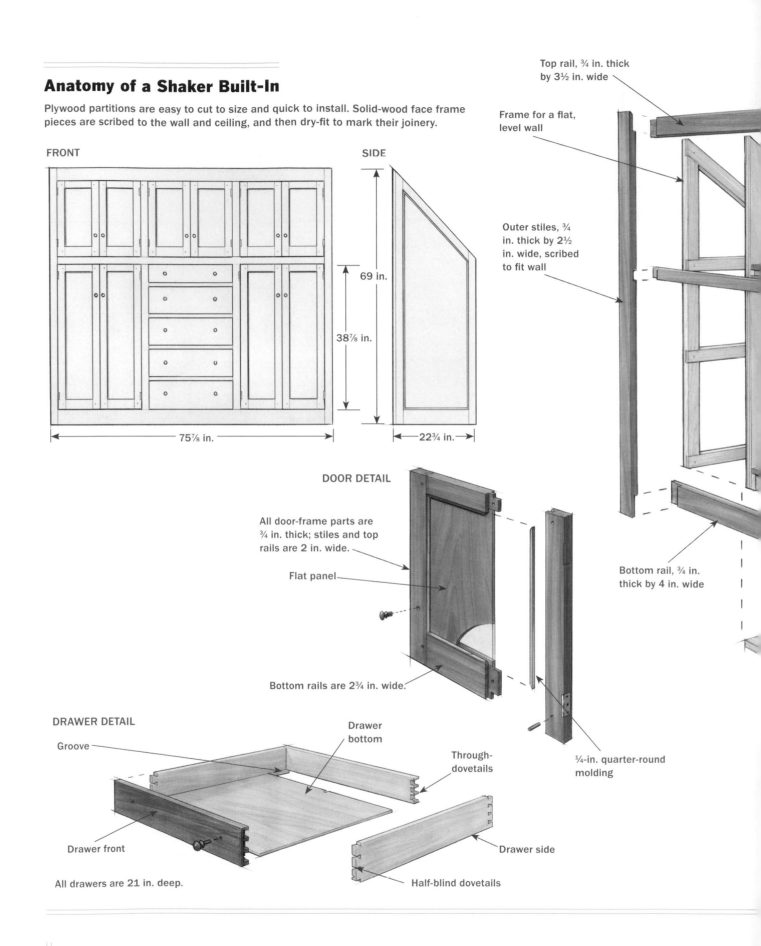

FRONT

SIDE

69 in.

38⅞ in.

75⅞ in.

22¾ in.

Top rail, ¾ in. thick by 3½ in. wide

Frame for a flat, level wall

Outer stiles, ¾ in. thick by 2½ in. wide, scribed to fit wall

Bottom rail, ¾ in. thick by 4 in. wide

DOOR DETAIL

All door-frame parts are ¾ in. thick; stiles and top rails are 2 in. wide.

Flat panel

Bottom rails are 2¾ in. wide.

¼-in. quarter-round molding

DRAWER DETAIL

Groove

Drawer bottom

Through-dovetails

Drawer front

Drawer side

Half-blind dovetails

All drawers are 21 in. deep.

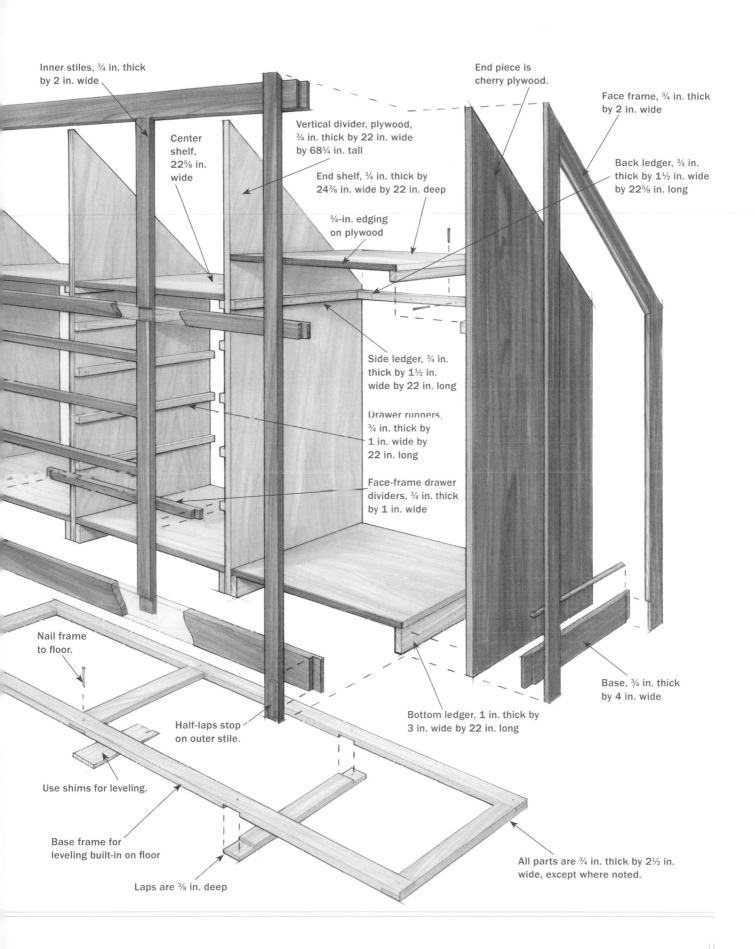

Inner stiles, ¾ in. thick by 2 in. wide

Center shelf, 22⅝ in. wide

Vertical divider, plywood, ¾ in. thick by 22 in. wide by 68¼ in. tall

End shelf, ¾ in. thick by 24⅜ in. wide by 22 in. deep

¼-in. edging on plywood

End piece is cherry plywood.

Face frame, ¾ in. thick by 2 in. wide

Back ledger, ¾ in. thick by 1½ in. wide by 22⅝ in. long

Side ledger, ¾ in. thick by 1½ in. wide by 22 in. long

Drawer runners, ¾ in. thick by 1 in. wide by 22 in. long

Face-frame drawer dividers, ¾ in. thick by 1 in. wide

Nail frame to floor.

Half-laps stop on outer stile.

Use shims for leveling.

Base frame for leveling built-in on floor

Laps are ⅜ in. deep

Bottom ledger, 1 in. thick by 3 in. wide by 22 in. long

Base, ¾ in. thick by 4 in. wide

All parts are ¾ in. thick by 2½ in. wide, except where noted.

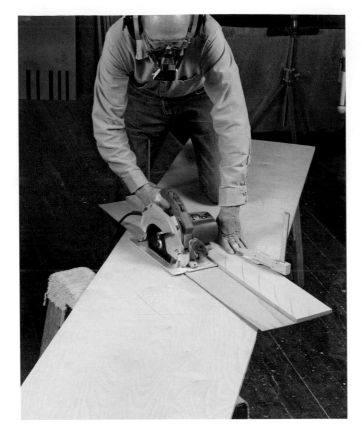

Vertical dividers are the backbone. Rip them to width, and then cut the 45° angle at the top using a circular saw and a simple cutting guide.

Troubleshoot the site

The more sound, plumb, and level the location, the easier your built-in construction and installation will be. The first thing to do is survey the site. If your walls and floors are old, warped, sloped, and out of square, then make leveling frames to fit the wall and the floor. Anything more than ⅛ in. is too much out of whack and you should correct for it. It takes some time and patience to get things just right, but the effort will be repaid with an easier construction and a straight and square finished product.

Mark the locations of your wall studs and use a level and shims to make sure the frame is plumb and flat. A stack of cedar shingles and a box of screws will allow you to shim those areas not making contact with the frame, all the while checking with the level. The same applies to the frame on the floor: It needs to be flat, level, and at 90° to the

wall. Again, shim and screw as needed. Remember, as you build the case you'll be toenailing the vertical dividers into the floor or floor frame, so you should strategically place the frame members to anticipate the locations of the dividers.

It's somewhat unconventional, but I installed my built-in over the carpeting. I prefer this to cutting out the carpet and padding under the built-in because cutting out a section and leaving the edges without a carpet strip holding them down could lead to buckling over time. The built-in is secured to the walls as well as the floor and the thin, firm carpet is a non-issue.

Get started on the vertical dividers

From my drawings, I knew I needed three sheets of ¾-in. birch plywood for the three walls, fixed shelves, bottoms, and sliding

shelves, and one sheet of cherry plywood for the visible exterior wall on the right. This wall will blend with all the solid-cherry door frames and the solid-cherry face frames.

I measured the height of the knee wall, located the wall studs, laid out the locations of the dividers, and drew the profile of the divider on the far left wall. With this information in hand, I returned to the shop and ripped the sheets of plywood in half. I cut one of the cherry and three of the birch half-sheets at 45° to make the two dividers and two end pieces.

Ledger strips keep it all together

Ledger strips make the construction straightforward, serving dual purposes: They give me a place to secure the bottoms and shelves, while locking everything together. The bottom ledgers rest on the floor or leveling frame and support the bottoms of the cabinets, while the upper ones hold the fixed shelf at the top of the knee wall. You'll nail through the bottom ledgers and leveling frame to lock the built-in to the floor.

From the leftover plywood, I cut three bottoms and three fixed shelves. All six pieces got ¼-in. cherry face strips glued to the front edge. On the undersides of the back of the three shelves, I glued and screwed ledger strips, allowing exactly ⅞ in. on both sides of the strip to leave room for the intersecting ledgers on the vertical dividers.

The installation begins with two types of frames

Although this is one large unit, I divided it in thirds and worked left to right, creating the first box and adding the shelf dividers to the box, then repeating the process for the next two sections (see the sidebar on pp. 104–105).

Build in place

This smart, easy installation method allows you to cut separate pieces in the shop and lock them into place on site. No need to lug cumbersome plywood boxes to and fro.

Create the first box by nailing the upper and lower shelves to their ledger strips (1). Set this box in place, nailing it to the side wall through the plywood divider. Finish by toenailing through the bottom ledger strip into the floor (2). Add a divider to create the next box. Again, nail the shelves to the ledger strips to hold it all together (3). As with the first box, the final step is to toenail through the bottom ledger strip into the floor.

Repeat the process. Work your way out, attaching the upper and lower shelves to each divider, and nailing it in the same way (4). Then secure the whole thing to the back wall by nailing through the ledger strips under the upper shelf. As always, predrill before nailing to prevent splitting (5).

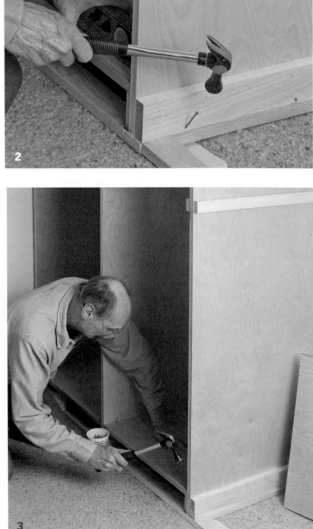

Spacer keeps the runners aligned. Rest the drawer runners on a simple spacing template as you nail them in place.

With the entire unit firmly anchored to the floor and back wall, I moved on to the face frames, but only after installing the drawer runners, which are just strips of solid wood. I used a plywood spacer block to make sure they are level and even on both sides (see the photo above).

It's the cherry exterior and solid-wood face frames, doors, and drawer faces that give this large plywood box its beauty and handcrafted look. The face frames are scribed to fit exactly into position; they also blend the transition from the walls, floor, and ceilings to the built-in. The right side of my built-in is exposed, so I needed to build a face frame and apply it to the plywood there. I also needed face frames around the front of the boxes. These cover the plywood and frame the doors and drawers.

An end cap on the end panel
Back in the shop, I made a cherry frame to go on the outside of the cherry end panel.

Scribe, fit, and glue the end cap in place.
To correct the small gaps on the end cap, run
a compass along the surface of the ceiling (1),
transferring the undulations to the frame stock.
Then use a block plane to shape the frame to
that line (2).

Fit the front edge too. Once the wall side of
the frame is profiled, set it in place and use the
plywood divider to run a line along the back side
of the end cap (3). Cutting to this line will make
sure the front is perfectly flush with the edge of
the plywood.

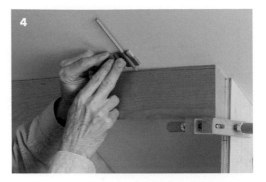

Fit and mark for the joints. After beveling the
edge of the top rail, set the rail in place, making
sure it is level. With a pencil on a block of wood,
scribe along the ceiling onto the rail (4), and then
trim to that line with a scrub plane or drawknife.

Work your way down. Starting with the top rail, tack the parts
in place with brads as you go (5). Move on to the frame stiles and
drawer dividers. Tack the stiles on top of the rails. The far right stile
is flush with the end cap. The center two are flush with the inside
walls of the center box, and the far left stile is flush with the wall
and may need scribing. Slide the drawer dividers behind the stiles
and clamp them to the drawer runners.

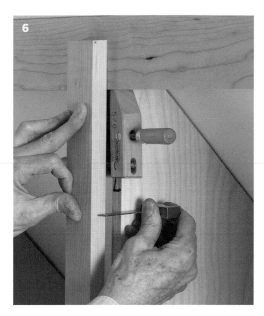

Mark all the intersections. Use a square and a marking knife to mark the intersections where you'll cut the lap joints (6). On ending intersections there will be four tick marks, and on crossings there will be eight tick marks (7).

The back and top portions of the frame are ¼ in. wider, with a back bevel, to be scribed to the ceiling and knee wall. To mimic the moldings on the doors, the interior edges of the end frame have ¼-in. quarter-round cherry moldings applied. While making up that molding, I routed and cut quarter-round moldings for all 10 doors yet to be built. When this end cap was built and scribed and planed to fit, I attached it. I glued the frame onto the end panel.

A real frame on the front

When the glue was dry on the end cap, I started on the face frames on the front edges of the built-in. These were milled to width and depth in the shop but left long. On site, I tacked them in place and marked them. The trick to a successful face frame is the order of operations and staying organized. Once everything is tacked in place, I make sure to mark the position of everything so I won't lose track of it.

With everything tacked in place, I used a sharp knife to make a tick mark where each member intersects, on both pieces. These tick marks indicate the locations of the lap joints.

Saw and rout the lap joints. Cut the shoulders with a handsaw (8), and then use a router to waste away the rest of the joint, working right up to the handsaw lines (9).

Then I took them back to the shop and cut the lap joints.

A versatile interior

After the built-in was constructed and before I finished it, I used a simple plywood jig to locate holes for shelf pegs, and drilled them with a cordless drill.

Nail the face frame in place. Reuse the nail holes from when you tacked up the frames (10). Start with any preassembled sections, and then add the individual pieces (11).

The last step is to make and fit the 10 doors and five drawers. I make traditional dovetailed drawers and run them on wooden runners, not commercial slides. I kept the face frames flush to the sides of the middle section with the drawers so I wouldn't have to block out for the drawers. The frame-and-panel doors are mounted with standard butt hinges, but I mortised them into the doors only. The hinges are surface-mounted to the frames.

Once the drawers are made and fitted and the doors are made, fitted, and hung, the entire piece can be finished. I used a mixture of Tried & True Varnish oil and spar varnish.

Assemble as much as possible in the shop. If you can move the frame to its location fully assembled, that's the best bet. But if low ceilings, staircases, and turning corridors prohibit that, assemble as much as you can in the shop and add the rest on site (12).

Mudroom Built-In

TONY O'MALLEY

An enclosed porch or mudroom can help keep dirt and snow from reaching the living areas of your house. It's also a great place to stow stuff you'd rather not have cluttering the kitchen or family room: boots, shoes, book bags, sports gear, and the like. But without designated storage areas, a mudroom becomes a minefield. An elegant solution is to make a built-in storage cabinet, which will not only look good and organize your life, but can also add value to your home.

This mudroom unit features a base cabinet topped with open locker-type cabinets. The base cabinet has a lift-lid section for stowing out-of-season stuff like winter boots.

Built-In Plans

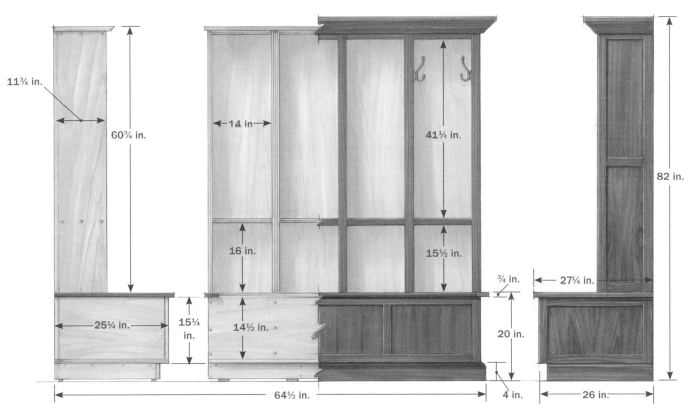

The upper cabinets have fixed shelves and hooks. This piece is designed for a family of four—with each person getting his or her own locker space—but it can be made larger or smaller to suit a different-size family.

The construction is simple: maple plywood cases with walnut face frames and applied frame-and-panel assemblies, which give the piece a furniture feel. Most of the parts are made in the shop and assembled on site.

Build the plywood boxes first

For this project, I used prefinished ¾-in.-thick maple plywood for all the cases. Though not commonly available at major home centers, the plywood often can be special-ordered at lumberyards. It saves you considerable finishing time, and creates a bright, durable interior that looks great with the dark walnut exterior.

Upper cabinet design

For the upper lockers (see pp. 112–113), I made four identical skinny cabinets and screwed them together. These smaller cabinets are easier to build, move around in the shop, and install. And this method can make the difference between needing a helper and getting the job done on your own. The plywood edges on the upper lockers are hidden with solid-walnut face frames, which are glued and nailed in place. To help align the face frames, I used ⅛-in.-thick splines cut

(continued on p. 115)

Clean cuts in plywood

When breaking down a full sheet of plywood on a tablesaw, rip the pieces to size, then crosscut them using a sled (1). To reduce tearout, keep the show face on top, and use a good combination blade and a zero-clearance insert or crosscut sled. To further reduce the chances of tearout during a crosscut, apply masking tape over the bottom side of the cut line (2).

Upper Cabinets Serve as Lockers

The top cabinets are individual plywood boxes screwed together and faced with solid walnut. These lockers have small cubbies for backpacks, purses, and briefcases, and larger spaces to hang coats and jackets.

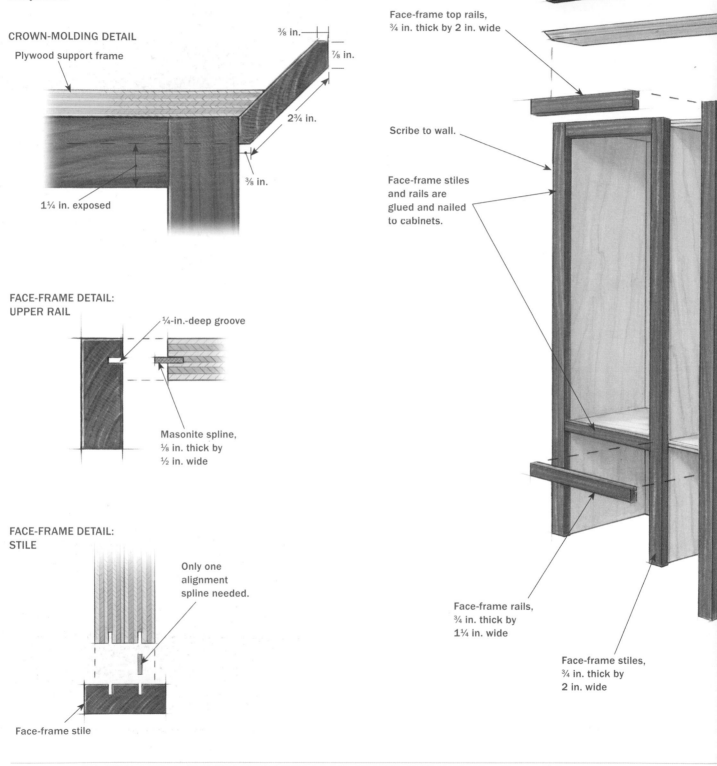

CROWN-MOLDING DETAIL

Plywood support frame

⅜ in.

⅞ in.

2¾ in.

⅜ in.

1¼ in. exposed

FACE-FRAME DETAIL: UPPER RAIL

¼-in.-deep groove

Masonite spline, ⅛ in. thick by ½ in. wide

FACE-FRAME DETAIL: STILE

Only one alignment spline needed.

Face-frame stile

Face-frame top rails, ¾ in. thick by 2 in. wide

Scribe to wall.

Face-frame stiles and rails are glued and nailed to cabinets.

Face-frame rails, ¾ in. thick by 1¼ in. wide

Face-frame stiles, ¾ in. thick by 2 in. wide

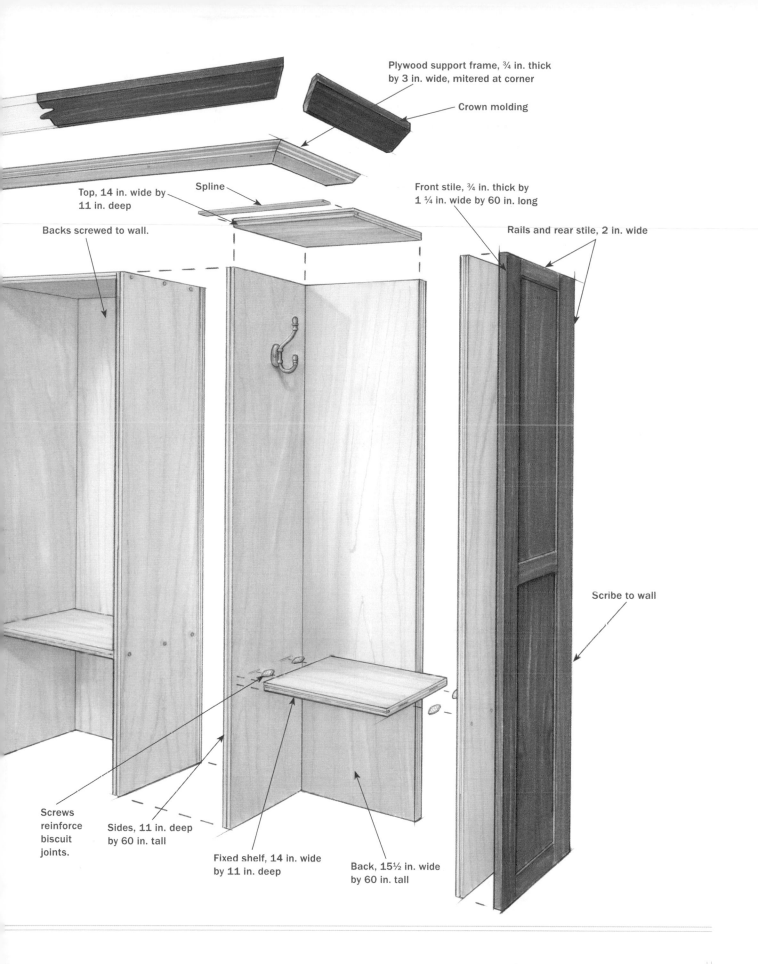

Plywood support frame, ¾ in. thick by 3 in. wide, mitered at corner

Crown molding

Top, 14 in. wide by 11 in. deep

Spline

Front stile, ¾ in. thick by 1 ¼ in. wide by 60 in. long

Backs screwed to wall.

Rails and rear stile, 2 in. wide

Scribe to wall

Screws reinforce biscuit joints.

Sides, 11 in. deep by 60 in. tall

Fixed shelf, 14 in. wide by 11 in. deep

Back, 15½ in. wide by 60 in. tall

Base Cabinet Offers Seating and Storage

The lower cabinet is a plywood box faced with walnut frames and panels. The height is perfect for sitting to change shoes, and the lidded box has plenty of room for items you don't want to see, like boots and outdoor gear.

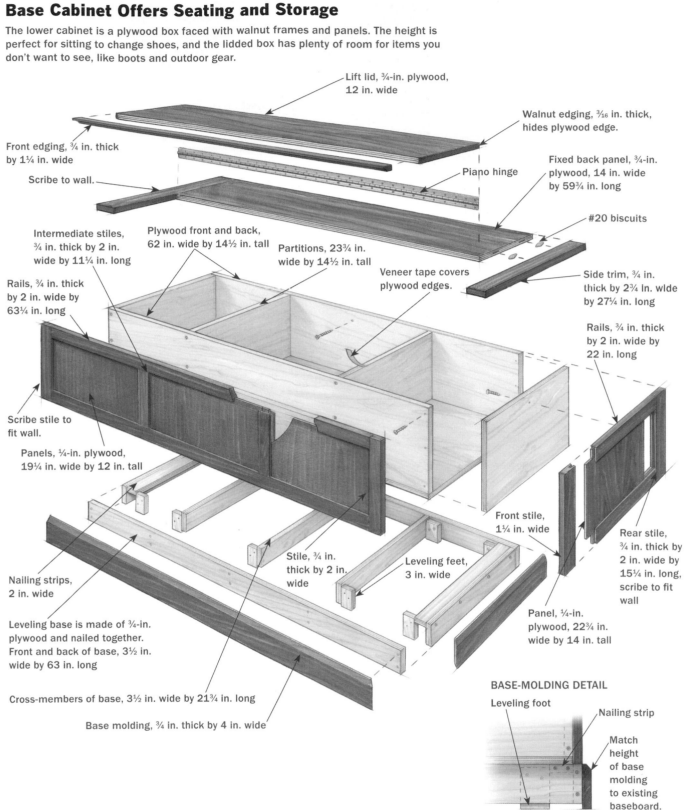

Lift lid, ¾-in. plywood, 12 in. wide

Walnut edging, ³⁄₁₆ in. thick, hides plywood edge.

Front edging, ¾ in. thick by 1¼ in. wide

Scribe to wall.

Piano hinge

Fixed back panel, ¾-in. plywood, 14 in. wide by 59¾ in. long

#20 biscuits

Intermediate stiles, ¾ in. thick by 2 in. wide by 11¼ in. long

Plywood front and back, 62 in. wide by 14½ in. tall

Partitions, 23¾ in. wide by 14½ in. tall

Veneer tape covers plywood edges.

Side trim, ¾ in. thick by 2¾ in. wide by 27¼ in. long

Rails, ¾ in. thick by 2 in. wide by 63¼ in. long

Rails, ¾ in. thick by 2 in. wide by 22 in. long

Scribe stile to fit wall.

Panels, ¼-in. plywood, 19¼ in. wide by 12 in. tall

Front stile, 1¼ in. wide

Rear stile, ¾ in. thick by 2 in. wide by 15¼ in. long, scribe to fit wall

Nailing strips, 2 in. wide

Stile, ¾ in. thick by 2 in. wide

Leveling feet, 3 in. wide

Leveling base is made of ¾-in. plywood and nailed together. Front and back of base, 3½ in. wide by 63 in. long

Panel, ¼-in. plywood, 22¾ in. wide by 14 in. tall

Cross-members of base, 3½ in. wide by 21¾ in. long

Base molding, ¾ in. thick by 4 in. wide

BASE-MOLDING DETAIL

Leveling foot

Nailing strip

Match height of base molding to existing baseboard.

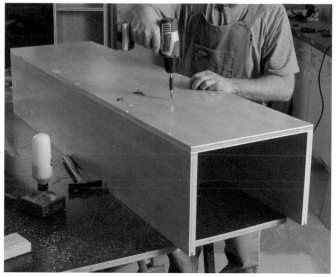

No clamps required. Assemble the shelves, top, and sides with biscuits and screws. The screws not only reinforce the biscuits, but they also eliminate the need for clamps. Drill clearance holes and countersinks in the top pieces, and pilot holes in the edges below to prevent splitting.

from tempered Masonite®. Before assembling the cases, I cut the grooves for the splines in all the front edges using a router and a slot-cutting bit. To assemble the cases, I used screws and biscuits.

Base cabinet design

The base cabinet goes together with the same biscuit-and-screw joinery as the locker cabinets. One difference is that I used an adhesive-backed maple edge-banding on the top edge of the two exposed partitions.

Put on the edge-banding before you cut the partitions to size. That way, the banded partitions don't vary in size from the un-banded ends of the case. Trim the edge-banding with a chisel.

Make and prefinish the walnut parts

Once the plywood cases are glued up, you can begin working on the walnut face frames, the frame-and-panel assemblies, and the lift-

lid assembly. All of the walnut parts should be finished (I used Minwax Wipe-On Poly) before installation. It's much easier that way.

Because most walls aren't square or flat, you'll need to fit the end pieces of the built-in to that irregular surface. So leave any piece that butts against the wall about ⅜ in. over-size in width (or length for the moldings) to allow for scribing and fitting.

Face frame

Mill the face-frame stock to thickness and width, but leave the pieces long. They'll be trimmed to fit the case during installation. That will leave the end grain unfinished, but no one will see it. I chamfer the edges and ends of every face-frame part to create a small V-groove at each intersection; this detail not only looks good but also masks any minor unevenness at the joints. You can't chamfer the ends now, because the pieces aren't cut to final length, but you should chamfer the edges and prefinish the pieces.

Fixed back gets solid edges. Attach the side trim pieces to the fixed back with biscuits.

Hide exposed edges on lid. The side edge-bandings are glued on with masking tape as the clamps, and the front edging is attached with biscuits. All the edging is trimmed flush with a block plane and cleaned up with sandpaper.

Soft landing for fingers. After gluing on the front edging and trimming it flush with the plywood, rout a cove along the bottom edge to serve as a finger pull.

Frame-and-panel assemblies

The front and exposed side of this built-in are covered with applied frame-and-panel assemblies made from solid walnut and ¼-in.-thick plywood and assembled with simple joinery.

Base and crown moldings

Like the face frames, both the base and crown molding are solid walnut. For efficiency, mill up both at the same time. The base molding has a simple beveled profile. It's a good idea to leave it a bit wider than its finished size and trim it to fit after installation. The crown molding also is simple.

All four bevel cuts are made with the tablesaw blade at 42°. Clean up any saw marks with a handplane or sandpaper. The miters and scribing are done during installation. To support the crown, I use a beveled plywood strip screwed to the top of the case. Cut the strip and bevel its edge.

Last, the lift lid

The top of the lower cabinet features a lift lid, a fixed back (on which the upper cabinets will sit), and two pieces of side trim. I decided to use ¾-in.-thick walnut plywood for the lid and fixed back to eliminate any wood movement worries. To ensure a good grain match, cut the fixed back and lid from one piece of plywood.

Assembly: Start with a level foundation

Built-in cabinetry must be installed level and plumb, no matter how out of whack the

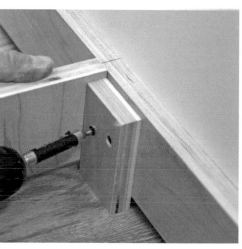

Add feet. Use shims to get the base perfectly level (left) and up to the target height. Once the base is at the target height, screw on the plywood feet (above).

Put the cabinet on the base. Screw it to the base and to the wall with finish-head screws. Shim behind the cabinet if the wall isn't plumb.

Side panel is next. Scribe the rear stile to the wall and trim the panel flush with the front of the cabinet. Screw it to the cabinet from inside.

Top it off. Place the fixed back panel on top and screw it to the lower cabinet from above. The screws will be hidden by the upper lockers.

Clamp and screw. Set the four locker cabinets in place and attach one to the next with countersunk drywall screws, which help draw the pieces together. Screw the cabinets to the wall, shimming the back where necessary to keep them plumb.

floors and walls may be. One of my favorite tricks is to install a separate base that can be leveled without moving the entire cabinet back and forth in the process (see the photos on p. 117). Once the base is complete, install the cases, starting with the lower cabinet and finishing with the upper lockers.

The upper cases are screwed to one another and to the wall. Then the side and front panels are scribed to the wall and screwed on from inside. If you don't like seeing screw heads inside the lockers, cover them with matching maple screw caps, available from Fastcap.

Scribe to the wall. Where the frames meet the wall, you need to create a seamless fit. The best approach is to set the panel in place and slide a light-colored pencil (which shows on the dark walnut) along the wall to mark its contours (left). Trim up to the line using a block plane, jigsaw, or belt sander (above). Your other goal is a flush surface at the front of the cabinet.

Hinge the lid. Screw the piano hinge to the lid, then attach the assembly to the fixed back.

Face frames without frustration. Rather than attaching a preassembled frame, the author glues and nails on the pieces one at a time, beginning with the verticals. Then he fits the horizontals.

The topper. To give a better attachment surface for the crown molding, nail on a plywood support piece along the edges (left). Then miter the crown, and glue and nail it in place (right).

Cover up the plywood edges

Now it's time to install the front frame-and-panel assembly, the lid, the face frames, and the moldings. Don't hurry these jobs, because these details are the most visible. The front is screwed to the lower case from the inside. The lid is attached to the fixed back with a piano hinge.

When gluing and nailing on the face-frame pieces, attach the verticals first and the horizontals last. Because they're for alignment only, you need only one spline per vertical piece, even though the three middle pieces cover two cabinet sides. Conceal the nail heads with a colored wax crayon.

On the horizontal frame pieces, remember to chamfer the ends, and apply finish to that small chamfer before installation.

Now all you have to do is install the crown molding and base molding. Once you're finished, you'll have a handy place to store all sorts of stuff, and a convenient seat where you can put on and take off shoes and boots.

A Clever Kitchen Built-In

NANCY R. HILLER

Modern kitchens are made for storage, but there never seems to be enough. Recently, my company built a cabinet to provide generous storage on a shallow section of wall in our clients' kitchen. It was space that normally would have gone to waste because it was too shallow for stock cabinets.

The inspiration for this custom-made cabinet came from a traditional piece of British furniture known as a Welsh dresser. In use since the 17th century, the dresser originally provided the main storage in a kitchen; built-in cabinets did not become the norm until the early 20th century. More commonly known in the United States by the less elegant term hutch, the dresser typically has a shallow, open upper section that sits on a partially enclosed base. The dresser described here also exemplifies the sort of planning, production, and installation needed for genuinely custom built-in cabinets.

A strategy for storage that doesn't waste space

The kitchen had a section of unused wall about 11 ft. long, which I thought could be used for storage and display space without impeding traffic flow. Although 1 ft. of depth is shallow for a base cabinet, it is enough to hold a surprising variety of kitchen wares: cookbooks, decorative china, coffee mugs, small mixing bowls, or jars of beans or pasta. Knowing that one of my clients had grown up in England and would be familiar with Welsh dressers, I suggested a similar cabinet with more contemporary lines, customized for her family's budget and for the available space.

The upper sections would have open shelves, but the base cabinets would be enclosed with doors and drawers to keep their contents free of the dust and debris that collect at a kitchen's edges. Enclosing the lower sections also would give a nice visual weight to the wall without making it appear too heavy. The break between base and upper cabinets would be at 32 in., not the typical kitchen-counter height of 36 in., because I wanted this piece to look more like furniture than a regular kitchen cabinet.

Building smaller components makes the project easier

The six-piece unit is divided into three uppers and three bases for ease of production, delivery, and installation (see the drawing on p. 123). To make the six plywood cases and the solid-maple counter resemble a single piece of cabinetry, I used a complete maple face frame on the center section of the upper and lower casework and a partial face frame on each end. The end cases would butt tightly against the center unit and share its face-frame stiles to make the unit appear as one piece (see the drawings on pp. 124–125).

Although 10-in. slides are available for many purposes and would have been ideal for this job, they are rated only for drawers up to approximately 2 ft. wide. For smooth operation, I needed hardware designed for oversize openings. Given the location of the adjacent door casing, which limited the cabinet's depth to a maximum of 12¾ in., and a design that called for inset drawer faces, we needed to create ¼ in. of additional depth to accommodate the 12-in. slides by routing out the plywood cabinet back in those locations.

For ease of production, I typically use a full-width applied back on built-in cabinets rather than rabbeting the cabinet sides to accept the back. Scribed on site, a finished end covers the seam between the cabinet and the ¼-in. back. After cutting biscuit slots to join the case sides to the tops, I used cleats fastened with glue and brads or screws to support the case bottoms. The biscuit- and cleat-supported butt joints were reinforced with 1½-in. screws after the casework was put together.

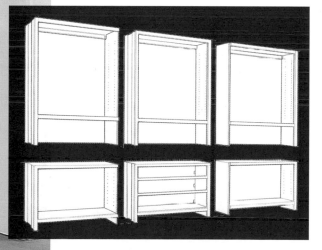

More parts make construction efficient. This type of modular cabinet construction allows a majority of the assembly work to be done in the shop. Consequently, you get more control over the processes and their costs.

Anatomy of a Built-In

Segmented construction let us assemble everything in the shop, break it down, and reassemble it in the kitchen. After the plywood boxes were screwed together in the shop, individual solid-wood face frames were glued to each box. The center cabinets had a complete face frame, while each side cabinet's frame, when joined to the center, would share the center's left or right stile.

At the house, we reassembled the base cabinets, shimmed them level, and screwed them to the framing. After scribing the counter to fit, we screwed it to the base cabinets. We installed the upper cabinets in the same way as the lower.

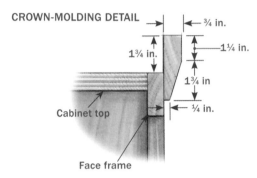

CROWN-MOLDING DETAIL

¾ in.

1¾ in.

1¼ in.

1¾ in

¼ in.

Cabinet top

Face frame

UNDERCOUNTER MOLDING DETAIL

Countertop

Oversize hole, ⁷⁄₁₆ in. dia., allows seasonal wood movement.

#8 by 1¼-in. screw

Fender washer

Face frame

Outer molding, ⅜ in. thick by ¾ in. wide

Base molding, ¼ in. thick by 1½ in. wide

FACE-FRAME DETAIL

Plywood spacer

Outer cabinet

Center cabinet

Outer face-frame rail

Middle face-frame stile

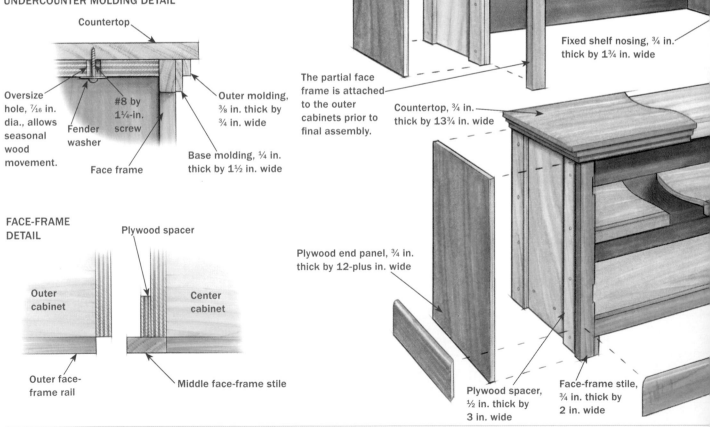

Fixed shelf nosing, ¾ in. thick by 1¾ in. wide

The partial face frame is attached to the outer cabinets prior to final assembly.

Countertop, ¾ in. thick by 13¾ in. wide

Plywood end panel, ¾ in. thick by 12-plus in. wide

Plywood spacer, ½ in. thick by 3 in. wide

Face-frame stile, ¾ in. thick by 2 in. wide

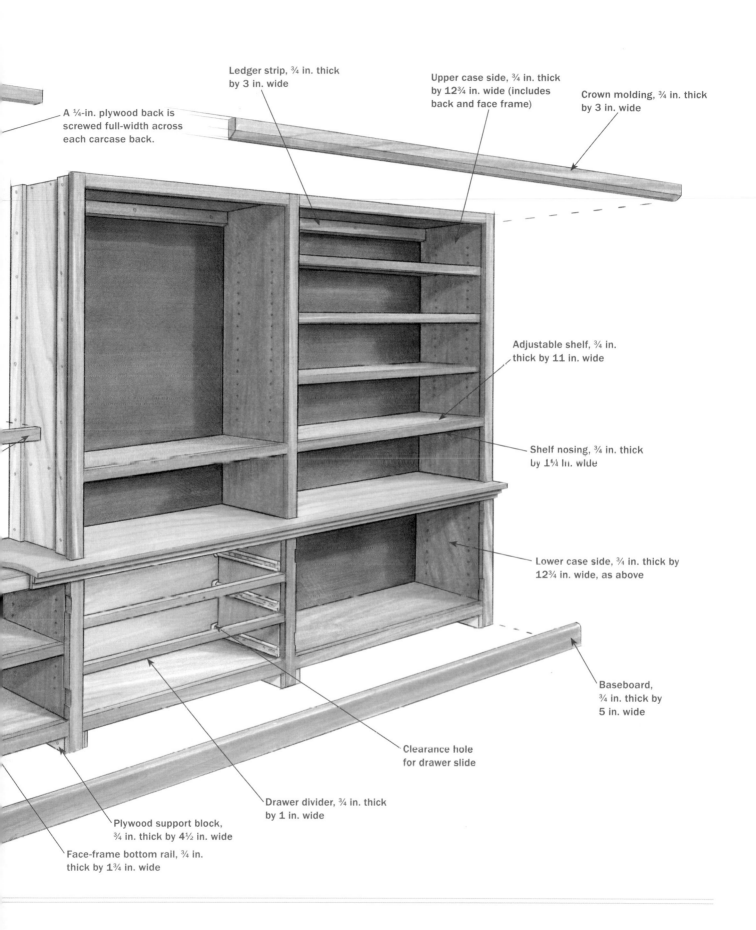

A ¼-in. plywood back is screwed full-width across each carcase back.

Ledger strip, ¾ in. thick by 3 in. wide

Upper case side, ¾ in. thick by 12¾ in. wide (includes back and face frame)

Crown molding, ¾ in. thick by 3 in. wide

Adjustable shelf, ¾ in. thick by 11 in. wide

Shelf nosing, ¾ in. thick by 1¼ in. wide

Lower case side, ¾ in. thick by 12¾ in. wide, as above

Baseboard, ¾ in. thick by 5 in. wide

Clearance hole for drawer slide

Drawer divider, ¾ in. thick by 1 in. wide

Plywood support block, ¾ in. thick by 4½ in. wide

Face-frame bottom rail, ¾ in. thick by 1¾ in. wide

First assembly is done in the shop for a better final fit. After cabinetmaker Jerry Nees glued the center face frame to the center cabinet, he clamped the base cabinets together in the shop (right). The left and right portions of the face frame then can be scribed to fit and glued to their respective cabinets (above). The process is repeated for the upper cabinets.

As we assembled the cases, I checked for square and twist. I also cleaned off squeezed-out glue before it dried.

Solid-wood parts need special consideration

Depending on the finish, I use either mortise-and-tenon joinery or pocket screws to assemble face frames before gluing them to carcases. Although pocket screws are quick and simple, I don't think the joint is as immobile as a glued mortise and tenon. While a hairline gap isn't as noticeable in natural wood, I've learned the hard way not to use pocket screws for painted work that needs to look seamless. For this project, after the face frames were pocket-screwed, we glued and clamped them to the carcases.

I made the solid-maple counter by edge-joining two or three full-length boards. To increase the glue surface and to keep the

boards even during clamping, I used biscuit joints about every 18 in. along the length. I figured the approximate location of the finished end so that I could avoid exposing a biscuit when I made the final cut. I sanded and finished counters in the shop before I scribed and installed them.

When I make cabinet doors, I keep the stock as thick as possible, at least ¾ in. and ideally ⅞ in. (see the drawing on the facing page). I flatten door stock on the jointer, then run it through the thickness planer to ensure that it is flat, square-edged, and uniformly thick. Using bar clamps rather than pipe clamps can help to keep doors flat. I lay the door directly on the clamp-bar surface so that I can detect any deflection, and I clamp the door to the bar using smaller clamps if necessary. I check for square by comparing diagonal measurements and hold a straight-edge across the top and bottom of the frame

Solid Details for Long-Lasting Doors

For most cabinet doors, I make stiles and rails from stock that's slightly thicker than ¾ in. I prefer to use mortise-and-tenon joinery (below), but cope-and-stick is also a viable option (bottom). I cut the grooves and tenons on the tablesaw, using a dado blade and (for the tenons) a sliding miter gauge. I use a ⁵⁄₁₆-in.-wide mortise-and-tenon joint; I have found that my mortising machine's ⁵⁄₁₆-in.-dia. auger bit and hollow chisel are less likely to break from overheating than are ¼-in. tools. My door panels are typically solid wood. If the groove is ½ in. deep, I make the panel ⅛ in. less all around to allow for some expansion. In summer, when the relative humidity is high here in Indiana, I make the panels extend closer to ⁷⁄₁₆ in. into a ½-in.-deep groove.

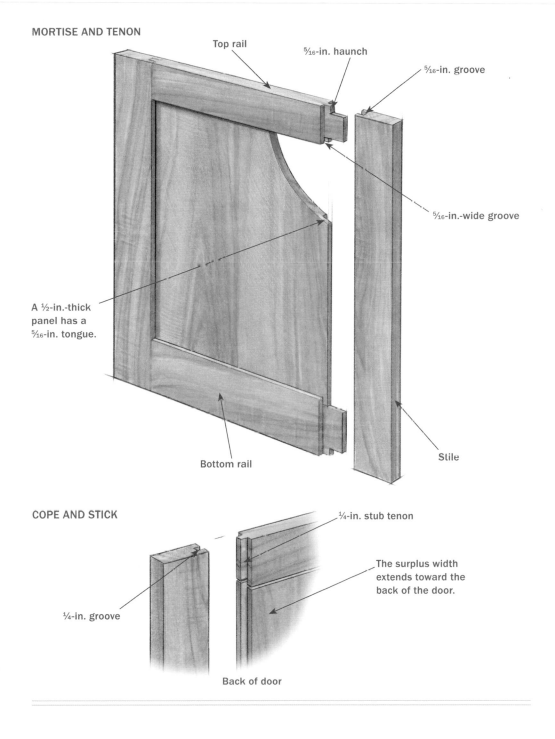

MORTISE AND TENON

Top rail

⁵⁄₁₆-in. haunch

⁵⁄₁₆-in. groove

⁵⁄₁₆-in.-wide groove

A ½-in.-thick panel has a ⁵⁄₁₆-in. tongue.

Bottom rail

Stile

COPE AND STICK

¼-in. stub tenon

The surplus width extends toward the back of the door.

¼-in. groove

Back of door

Drawer construction and installation

I usually make drawers from ½-in. solid stock and dovetail the corners; it's a joinery option that my customers expect. (For less-expensive projects, I use biscuits or a rabbeted joint, as shown in the detail drawings on the facing page). I groove the inside faces of the front and sides to accept the drawer bottom (I use ⅜-in.- or ½-in.-thick plywood for the bottoms of extra-wide drawers to prevent them from sagging). I also rip the back even with the top face of the drawer bottom so that I can slide in the bottom once the drawer sides are glued.

A drawer that's 40 in. wide requires special slides to withstand the stresses that are placed on it when it's fully extended. However, the full-extension, heavy-duty 12-in. drawer slides from Accuride® (www.accuride.com) that I chose turned out to be ¼ in. longer than the inside of the base cabinets. Fortunately, cutting a hole in the cabinet's back (see the photo below left) made just enough space.

To install the drawers, I hang the drawer box first and then apply the face later (see the drawing on the facing page). Typically, I hang the drawer box with special low-profile screws that can be purchased with the drawer hardware. The drawer box should be hung initially about ⅛ in. behind its final position. In this instance, however, I was working with ¾-in.-thick applied drawer faces, so the box was set back ⅞ in.

Securing the bottom with small screws (but no glue) provides the option of a removable drawer bottom.

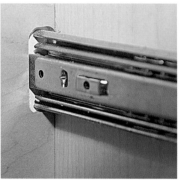

Wide drawers need special hardware, but to make it fit I had to cut holes in the cabinet's back.

to ensure that the rail and stile joints are glued up flat, not bowed. I also check for twist, either by sighting across the bare surface of the door or with the aid of winding sticks. Finally, I check the back of the door to make sure the panel is centered in the frame, and I adjust it if necessary by applying pressure with a wide chisel.

When the doors are dry, I rough-fit them to the cabinet openings using a handplane or a tablesaw. Then I rout and chisel mortises for the butt hinges on the cabinets' face frames; the mortises in the doors will come later.

Next, I install the case backs and the solid ledgers. These hanging strips are screwed not just through the ¼-in. plywood cabinet backs, but directly through the top, the sides, or both. If the strips go through only the back and the back should somehow detach from the case, the entire assembly can fall forward, causing damage and possibly injury.

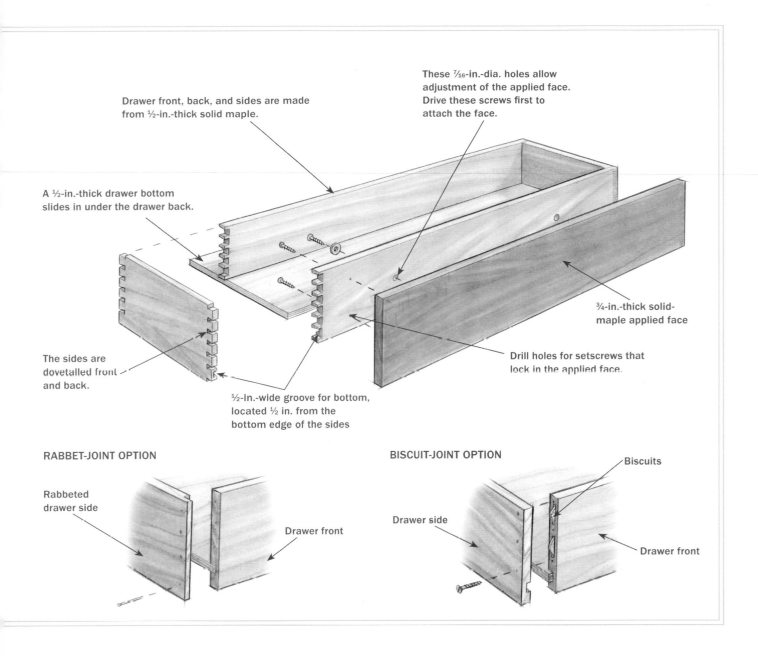

These 7/16-in.-dia. holes allow adjustment of the applied face. Drive these screws first to attach the face.

Drawer front, back, and sides are made from ½-in.-thick solid maple.

A ½-in.-thick drawer bottom slides in under the drawer back.

¾-in.-thick solid-maple applied face

The sides are dovetailed front and back.

Drill holes for setscrews that lock in the applied face.

½-in.-wide groove for bottom, located ½ in. from the bottom edge of the sides

RABBET-JOINT OPTION

Rabbeted drawer side

Drawer front

BISCUIT-JOINT OPTION

Biscuits

Drawer side

Drawer front

Installation starts at the highest point of the floor

Because this design called for an applied base molding, I could shim the casework up to level and count on the baseboard to hide the shims. I began from the high point on the floor and shimmed the cases as necessary. The sections also were clamped together, so I could treat the three cabinets as a unit if the wall behind them wasn't flat.

I use solid wood for counters because it generally holds up better than plywood and looks better with wear. When a solid counter is attached to a plywood case, the wood has to be able to move with changes in relative humidity. I set the counter in place and scribe as necessary, then attach it with screws in oversize holes that allow for wood movement.

As with the bases, I scribe the right face-frame stile to conform to irregularities in the wall, then screw together the upper units to form a single assembly before attaching it to the rear wall. No shimming is necessary because these upper cases are placed on a surface that should be level. I scribe the finished ends as needed and glue them in place. I also sand the face-frame edges flush if necessary.

Hang the doors and drawers after the casework is locked in

After applying the baseboard and crown molding, I work on the doors. For inset applications, I like to plane doors and drawer faces to size after installing the casework. Although this technique is unconventional, I find it more efficient. Once in their final position, cabinets don't always sit quite the way they did in the ideal conditions of the shop, so postponing this final fitting until the installation is complete means the work is done only once.

After shimming the doors in place with the proper margins (about $\frac{3}{32}$ in. for stain grade, more for painted work), I mark the positions of the hinge mortises on the door stiles. Once marked, the door is clamped in a vise or on sawhorses, where I rout the mortises and mount the hinges. Once the door is rehung, I do a final fitting with a handplane.

Setting the drawers is the final stage. After finalizing the fit, I use a pair of screws and fender washers to hold the drawer face in position. Once I'm satisfied with the fit, I drive in four additional screws to lock the face to the drawer box.

Built-Ins, Anywhere

GARY STRIEGLER

Even if you live in a place where it's 80°F and sunny all the time, you probably still need a mudroom. It's like an air lock in a spaceship, a transition area between the outside and the inside. A well-designed mudroom should have space to store coats, backpacks, boots, and everything

A dedicated space for everyone. Coats can be hung from pegs. Adjustable shelves offer space for items used less often. The shelves also can be used to display objects. The counter is a convenient place for dropping briefcases, books, keys, and cell phones. Below, a drawer and a pair of doors provide concealed storage. An 18-in.-high seat makes a convenient place to change shoes. Shoe and boot storage is directly below.

Built-In Plan

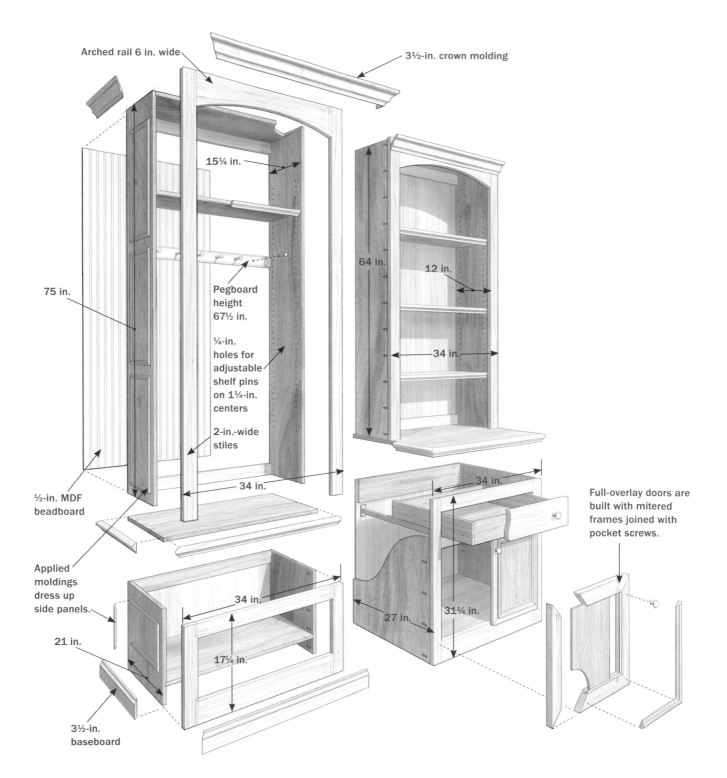

Arched rail 6 in. wide

3½-in. crown molding

15¼ in.

64 in.

12 in.

75 in.

Pegboard height 67½ in.

¼-in. holes for adjustable shelf pins on 1¼-in. centers

2-in.-wide stiles

34 in.

½-in. MDF beadboard

Applied moldings dress up side panels.

21 in.

3½-in. baseboard

34 in.

17¼ in.

34 in.

27 in.

31¼ in.

Full-overlay doors are built with mitered frames joined with pocket screws.

Build the boxes. First, cut plywood parts to size with a track saw.

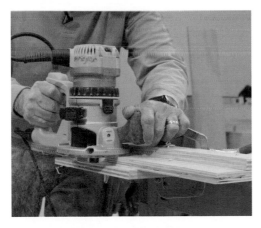

With a straight router bit and fence, cut ⅛-in. by ¾-in. dadoes in the cabinet side to house the top and bottom pieces, followed by ¾-in. by ½-in. dadoes on each piece to receive the plywood back.

else that family members use on a daily basis. It also should be a comfortable place where you can complete the last steps of dressing before facing the outside world.

Mudrooms are usually shared spaces, but when I build them, I like to provide some personal storage space for each family member—and still keep it out in the open. After all, it's a lot harder to forget something when it's right in front of you. I also think it's important to have some concealed storage for things such as umbrellas that you don't

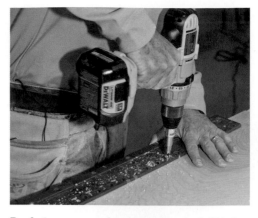

Pocket screws make strong boxes. Drill holes for adjustable shelf pins (above) and pocket holes (center), including those meant to attach the face frames.

need every day. When shelving is part of my storage design, I make it adjustable. There is no telling what you'll need to store down the road. Finally, I want every mudroom to have some counter space for things like cell phones, keys, and books.

Built in the shop, on site

When I build a cabinet on site, I use the same basic methods that I would use in a shop. I build the cabinet boxes, attach face frames, then screw the boxes to the wall and to each other. To do this, I employ a few special tools to create a mini-shop. My track saw lets me cut sheet goods in a fairly tight space, and because the saw moves instead of the plywood, it's a one-man job. When cutting sheet goods with a tablesaw, I need a total of 20 ft. of space. With a track saw, I need about 10 ft. The only drawback is that I have to measure and mark each piece when I'm making multiple cuts.

When I'm building cabinet boxes, accuracy and strength are important. Kreg® Tool Company's Foreman makes fast work of drilling the pocket holes I use for joining cases and face frames (see the above photos center and right). Unlike the company's pocket-screw

Assemble and attach the face frame

Gluing and clamping face frames to cabinets takes time. Attaching face frames with nails creates holes that must be filled. Pocket screws (1) don't require long clamping time, and they create a fast and positive joint both for assembling and attaching the face frames. Face-frame joints are typically concealed (2), but in certain situations (3), visible holes can be filled with Kreg's proprietary dowel plugs (4, 5).

jig, this machine is self-contained and drills pilot holes with a lever-actuated indexing mechanism. The screws give me a strong joint without a lot of nail holes on the sides of the cabinet, and they pull the joints tight without clamps. Pocket-screw joints are more efficient than biscuit joints because you machine only one of the two pieces being joined. There are no problems with alignment and there's no clamp time. As soon as the screw is driven, I can move to the next step.

My miter saw sits in a homemade stand that has wide outfeed surfaces and a built-in clamp to hold my work if I need to use

Assemble the boxes. Clamp the pieces together and secure them with screws.

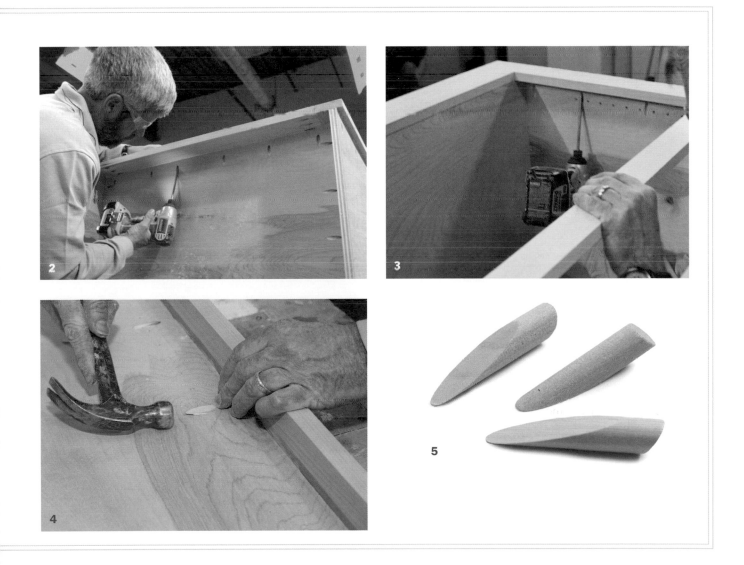

Install from the ground up

Base cabinets are installed first and should be shimmed level. Marking the location of framing in the wall makes it easier to screw cabinets to the studs. Any hollows in the wall should be shimmed out to prevent distortion of the cabinet backs when the screws are tightened (1). The first upper cabinet is placed on the base. Note that the base counter is attached to the upper cabinet first so that the exposed joint is as tight as possible. Trim screws join the two cabinets to each other and to the framing (2). Whenever possible, locate screws behind face frames or other less visible spots. Clamps provide a third hand to keep the joint tight between two cabinets while driving in screws (3). After the boxes have been assembled, the crown molding, baseboard, and other trim can be installed (4).

planer to remove saw kerfs from the edges of the lumber after it is ripped. (Always remember to rip pieces about ⅛ in. wider than you need so that the edges can be cleaned up.) A small tablesaw will do everything that I need done on the job site as long as I pair it with a good outfeed table that doubles as my main workbench.

Installing square boxes in an unsquare world

The installation process marries the measured geometry of the boxes to the often irregular condition of the room. If you are setting upper and lower cabinets separated by a backsplash, it's almost always easier to set the uppers first. However, in this mudroom, the uppers sit on base cabinets that must be installed first. I always start base-cabinet installation by checking the floor for level. I prefer to set cabinets at the highest corner and then shim everything else up to that point. If I can't start at the highest point, I carry the high point around the room and shim the first cabinet up to it. If the finished floor hasn't been installed, I add shims so that there are no problems when installing appliances after the floor is down.

It's also a good idea to check walls for plumb and to use a straightedge to check for humps. Bows or dips across the face of the wall will wreck a nice straight line of upper cabinets, so the cabinets may have to be shimmed out to keep the front edge straight.

When I cut the backs of cabinets for wiring or electrical boxes, I work from the side that will give the cleanest cut on the visible side. I also make allowances for out-of-plumb walls and factor in the amount of face-frame hangs beyond the sides of the plywood box. Remember, too, that a pilot hole is a great idea if you're screwing face frames together.

Bottoms up. The upper cabinet sits on the base cabinet, so you must install the base cabinet first.

the stand as a secondary workbench. Most important, it has an adjustable-stop system so that I can make accurate repetitive cuts of face-frame and door parts.

Most cabinet shops are set up around a large tablesaw and a heavy-duty planer. Because all my lumber is surfaced before it comes to the job site, I need only a portable

Maximize Pantry Storage

REX ALEXANDER

The minute I walked into Judy and Carl Rawski's home, I could tell they were tidy people. Not a thing was out of place. They both talked about how they had revamped many of their kitchen-cabinet interiors to make them more efficient but were stumped when it came to a closet they had designed at the end of a cabinet run. Frustrated with the usual wire shelving or boards resting on cleats, they were looking for lots of storage that was accessible, easy to clean, and attractive.

I like simplicity when designing a pantry, so I came up with the idea of building a closet-size cabinet to eliminate wasted space. Shallow drawers installed at various heights inside the cabinet would span the opening and make stored items easy to reach.

Prepare the closet for the cabinet

I wanted to use all the available space in the closet but still have the pullout shelving slide past the butt-hinged doors, even if they were opened only 90°. This meant the cabinet sides would need to be about 1½ in. inside the existing door jambs (see the drawing on the facing page). To inset the cabinet, I used 2x2 blocking at the front and 2x4 blocking at the

Stop diving deep to find the soup. Replace shelves with shallow drawers to make accessing items easier.

A Closetful of Pullouts

The simplest approach was to build a plywood cabinet, or box, that slid into the closet. Tongue-and-rabbet joints made assembly of such a big box easier because they kept the corners aligned. This same joint also can be used on drawers (see the sidebar on p. 140).

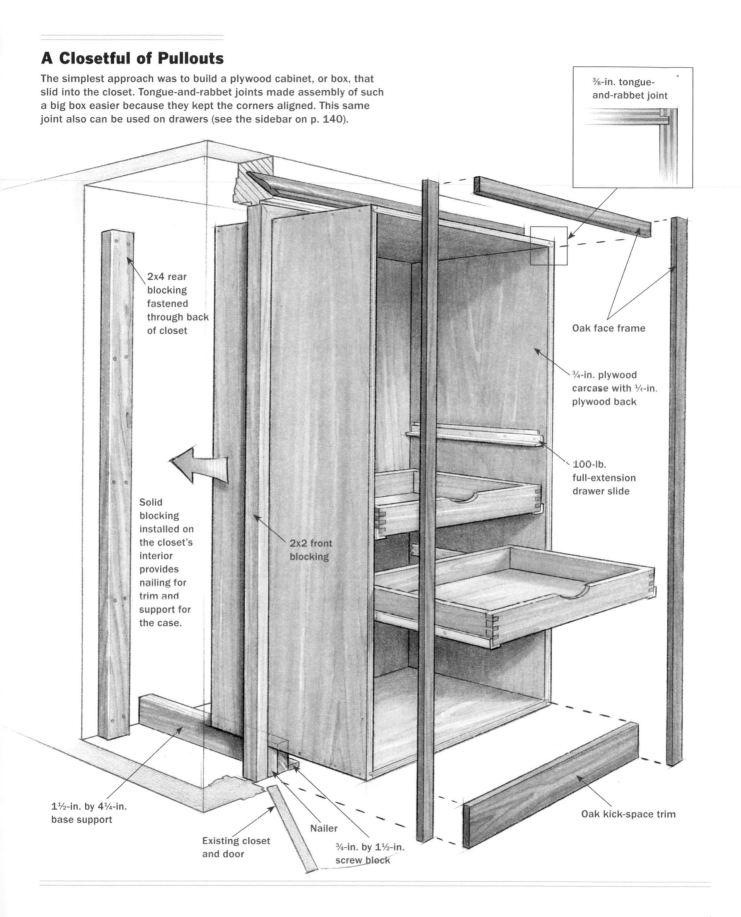

3/8-in. tongue-and-rabbet joint

2x4 rear blocking fastened through back of closet

Oak face frame

3/4-in. plywood carcase with 1/4-in. plywood back

100-lb. full-extension drawer slide

Solid blocking installed on the closet's interior provides nailing for trim and support for the case.

2x2 front blocking

1 1/2-in. by 4 1/4-in. base support

Existing closet and door

Nailer

3/4-in. by 1 1/2-in. screw block

Oak kick-space trim

Three drawer variations

You have your choice of different joinery options for the drawers.

Bottom pin wider to hide drawer bottom

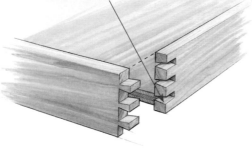

DOVETAILS
The drawers shown in the photo on p. 138 were built of solid maple with hand-cut dovetail joints, which are almost as labor-intensive as they are good-looking. The scooped fronts were cut with a bandsaw and sanded smooth. The drawer bottoms were made of ½-in. plywood glued into a ⅜-in. by ½-in. rabbet.

TONGUE AND RABBET
I've used this joint on drawers made from ½-in. Baltic-birch plywood. It's easily cut with a dado cutter in a tablesaw. Rout the rabbet for the bottom after assembling the drawer sides, front, and back.

BISCUITS
The third variation is also made from ½-in. Baltic-birch plywood, but has mitered corners that are joined with 0-size biscuits. The biscuit joiner must be kept square to the stock when cutting, or the miter will be offset.

back of the closet, which left enough room for a 32-in.-wide carcase.

I also installed blocking against the door's head jamb so that the cabinet's head casing would match the sides. On the closet floor, I attached ¾-in. by 1½-in. screw blocks perpendicular to the front edge, followed by two 4 ¼-in.-tall base supports. Smaller blocks served as nailers for the side casings.

Cut the parts, finish, then assemble

The Rawskis' kitchen cabinets have maple interiors, so I used maple plywood for the pantry closet. After I cut the parts, I put a dado head in my tablesaw and cut the tongue-and-rabbet joints for the carcase.

I finished all the parts before assembly. After taping off the areas to be glued, I lightly sanded all the surfaces with 220-grit sandpaper, then applied a satin polyurethane with a fine-nap roller. Two coats adequately protect the wood and give the surface a nice

sheen. The finish levels out perfectly, and roller marks disappear. After removing the tape from the joints, I applied glue, clamped together the pieces, and nailed the joints for insurance. Squaring up the carcase was easy once the ¼-in. plywood back was fastened in place.

Install and trim the unit

I mounted all the drawers with Blum® 550-mm epoxy-coated drawer slides (blum.com). They handle up to 100 lb., are easy to install, and operate smoothly.

The carcase slid into place along the base supports and between the blocking. I screwed the carcase to the blocking at the front and back of the closet. Then I nailed quartersawn oak trim flush with the inside edge of the cabinet; the trim floats on the outside edge for expansion and contraction. Finally, I filled the nail holes in the trim and installed the drawers onto the slides.

Taming an Outdated Pantry

JOSEPH LANZA

When we first started remodeling our house, space and time were tight. After I carved out a small office behind the kitchen, I was left with a space about 5½ ft. by 7½ ft. to serve as the laundry, the pantry, and a broom closet. We put a stacked washer/dryer in the corner by the kitchen door. On the wall next to it, I hung some heavy-duty wire shelving above the litter box. On the opposite wall, I built some plywood shelves to hold cans and boxes of food. This system worked while we readied an addition.

When the addition was complete, the laundry moved out, and more recycling boxes and wire shelving moved in. We knew we could do a lot more with the space. After eight or nine years of thinking about it, we had a pretty good idea of what we wanted, so I started modeling the pantry in SketchUp. An additional sink to handle houseplants and cleaning was first on the wish list. Recycling was next. I've built or installed a few kitchen-cabinet recycling centers, but they all have required transferring recyclables to another container on the way to the street. I liked the simplicity of tossing the stuff right into the curbside container. I didn't see why it wouldn't work inside a cabinet, preferably under the sink.

I brought the wall cabinets right up to the sloped ceiling. I knew this wouldn't get us much more usable space and also would make building the cabinets a bit more complicated, but it would get me out of building a soffit.

A scrap of plywood becomes a layout tool

After figuring out the basic design in SketchUp, I worked out the final dimensions at full scale using a story stick that I made from a scrap piece of plywood about 2 in. wide, cut to fit exactly between the walls of

Cabinets don't make the space bigger, but they do add efficiency and appeal. Formerly a cramped storage space (above), the pantry was transformed into a good-looking room with lots more storage by the addition of well-designed, simple, and elegant cabinets.

Squeezing the Most from 40 Sq. Ft.

NEW UPPER CABINETS
Instead of the usual 12-in.-deep uppers, the author made the new cabinets 16 in. deep. They can store a lot of stuff (serving bowls, lunch boxes, coolers, big wine bottles laid on their sides) that would never fit in a standard wall cabinet, as well as dishes and glassware.

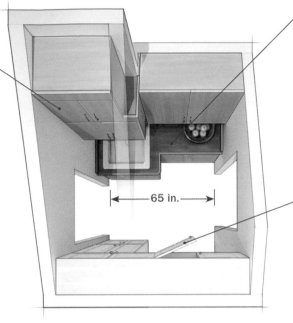

← 65 in. →

NEW BASE CABINETS
The finished-maple plywood cabinet boxes were assembled with butt joints, glue, and screws. The width of the sink base, 30½ in., was limited by the swing of the exterior door. To make sure that the recycling bin would fit underneath, the author made the base cabinets 27 in. deep and pushed the sink slightly off center. Now that the bin had a place, he could use the other 32-in.-wide base cabinet for drawers, which offer much more efficient storage than shelves.

DOORS FOR EXISTING SHELVES
The paint-grade cabinets use the wall space between the kitchen and office doors, including the space over the office door. They contain adjustable shelves used to store canned and dry goods, and at 12 in. deep, they don't interfere with traffic flow.

the spaces. Starting with the base cabinets, I held the stick in place and marked the edge of the plumbing pipes running on the outside of the left-hand wall, then opened the back door to see how much room I had for the sink base. I added a couple of inches beyond the swing of the door for the end panel and the countertop overhang, then marked out the cabinet between those marks on the stick. For the upper cabinets, I turned the same story stick over and held it against the back wall. I marked the corner where the wall jogs, then laid out the cabinets to the left and right. I drew all the components—cabinet sides, spacers, blocks, and scribe strips—on the story stick, then used the story stick (instead of my tape measure) to mark the plywood when I cut out the cabinet parts.

Build and hang the uppers first

I bought finished maple plywood for the cabinet boxes. It's pricey, but it also saves lots of time that would be spent applying finish. I built the uppers first because it was easier to install them without climbing over the base cabinets. The cabinet carcases are simple four-piece boxes (no backs) with the sides angled to follow the ceiling. I used a plunge router and a shop-made jig to drill holes for adjustable shelving, then assembled the boxes. Instead of plywood backs, I attached a poplar cleat at the back to attach the box to the wall and let the face frame square up the box. The lack of a back doesn't weaken the box, makes construction and installation easier, and in the case of the base cabinets, makes the integration of plumbing and other obstacles simpler.

Upper Cabinets

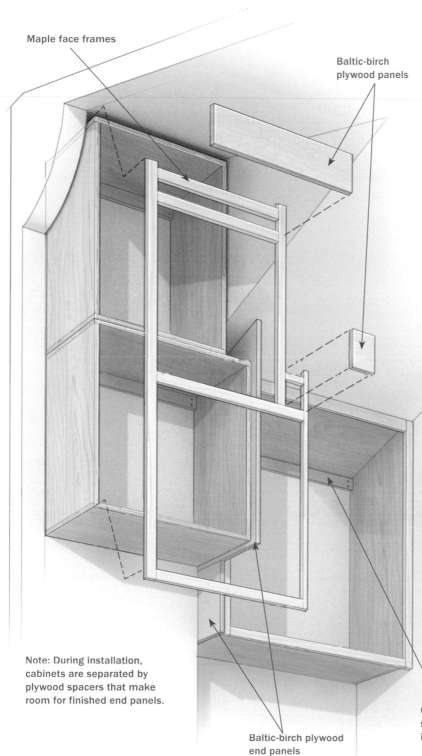

Maple face frames

Baltic-birch plywood panels

Note: During installation, cabinets are separated by plywood spacers that make room for finished end panels.

Baltic-birch plywood end panels

Cabinet boxes are screwed through cleats into the wall framing.

Check your work.
A handy layout and construction tool to use on jobs like this project, a story stick is a length of plywood scrap on which room measurements are recorded and cabinet spacing is determined. Once the cabinets are installed, use the stick to double-check their locations.

Assemble the face frames ahead of time.
Built in the shop with pocket screws, the frames are scribed to the wall and nailed to the boxes as units.

Lower Cabinets

A separate base is easy to level. In older houses, it's often easier to build and install separate bases for the lower cabinets. Basically plywood boxes, the bases are shimmed level and attached to the floor.

A great reason for backless cabinets. A backless cabinet can be placed and easily scribed to any protruding plumbing or wiring. The base cabinets are sized to create a traditional 3-in.-deep kick space below. Once the cabinets are attached to the base, the face frames are applied.

Systematic approach to drawer slides. Allow ¼-in. clearance between drawer fronts. Mark drawer-bottom locations on the inside cabinet wall, then transfer these marks to a piece of plywood. Use this piece inside the cabinet to support the top drawer slides while they're being attached to the cabinet sides.

Plywood strips attached to the top of the cabinets support the countertop.

Cabinet boxes are secured to bases and screwed through cleats into the wall framing.

Cabinet side is notched for plumbing.

Kick-face corner is mitered.

Baltic-birch plywood end panel

Even plywood can look good. The exposed laminations of the Baltic-birch plywood used for the doors and drawer fronts become a minimal design element.

I find it much easier to apply finished end panels after installation than to make the cabinets with finished sides, so during installation, I used ¾-in. spacers between the cabinets. I made the face frames from ¾-in. maple, joined with pocket screws. After hanging the boxes, I attached the face frames with glue and nails.

Next, install the kick base

I've found that it's less of a headache to build a plinth or kick base for cabinets, especially in an older house. Once the kick faces are shimmed level and attached to the floor, I can cover them with a clean piece of finished plywood that hides the shims and screwheads.

After building the boxes, I nailed them to the bases and screwed them to the walls. When all the cabinets were installed, I applied a shellac-based sanding sealer for color and finished with two coats of water-based polyurethane.

Drawers and doors complete the project

Rather than make frame-and-panel doors and drawers, I made them from ¾-in. Baltic-birch plywood. It's less expensive, and I like the minimalist look. After slightly rounding over the edges and finishing them, I hung the doors with clip-on full-overlay hinges. I drilled the 35-mm holes with a drill press equipped with a fence.

For the drawers, I used side-mounted ball-bearing slides. To simplify layout and to speed up installation, I like to align the bottom of the drawer box with the bottom of the drawer slide when it is mounted on the cabinet. Once I had laid out the drawer heights on the inside of the cabinet, I used a piece of plywood cut to the proper height to support each slide as it was installed. Start with the greatest distance, then cut the plywood down to the next drawer-slide height for each successive drawer. For the bottom drawer, rest the slide on a scrap of ¼-in. plywood on the bottom of the cabinet.

TIP Instead of creating a seam between the laminate and counter's edge, attach the edging first, then apply the laminate, letting it run over the edge. After the adhesive dries, bevel both laminate and edging with one router pass.

New doors dress up old shelves. Bare shelving (above) needed more than face frames. Rather than use clear-finished doors, the author milled cope-and-stick frames, then used ½-in. MDF beadboard for the panels (right).

Door Construction

Poplar frames are ¾ in. by 2½ in. with a cope-and-stick profile.

½-in. MDF beadboard panel, rabbeted ¼ in. by ⅜ in. to fit frame profile

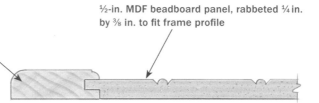

Paint-grade cabinets began as basic shelves

I had originally built a 24-in.-wide by 80-in.-high shelving unit out of ¾-in. lauan. The top extended over the door to the opposite wall, supported in the back by the head casing and on the wall by a small cleat. It had a nailed-on poplar face frame and a few pine shelves supported with pins. To make the shelves easily adjustable (and to avoid having to paint the inside of the cabinets), I made new faces for the sides from ¼-in. finished maple, drilling holes for adjustable shelves, then

gluing and nailing them over the existing cabinet sides. I also covered the shelves with the same ¼-in. plywood.

I hadn't considered doors before, but now that the other side of the pantry was closed in, open shelves didn't look right.

For the doors, I made poplar frames with ½-in. medium-density fiberboard (MDF) beadboard panels. Painted white, the cabinets combine with the new clear-finished cabinets to become an extension of the Baltic-birch and painted-beadboard cabinets in the kitchen.

Add Storage to Your Stair Rail

SCOTT GIBSON

My friend Kevin took a long look at the makeshift railing at the top of the stairs and hesitated only slightly before asking, "Have you thought about turning that into a bookcase?" It was not so much a question but rather a suggestion I recognized immediately as requiring a ton of extra work. But it was also too good to ignore. My wife's home office is right next to the stairwell, and by substituting a bookcase for a traditional balustrade, I could provide lots of storage for books and office supplies.

I sketched some ideas until I arrived at one I liked. Facing my wife's work area, the cabinet would have two sections of open shelves for books flanked by cabinets concealed with doors. A frame-and-panel back would face the stairs. To save a few inches of floor space, the case would overhang the stairwell, resting on a ledger and a series of brackets.

The bookcase gives us 18 running ft. of shelf space, plus two cabinets nearly 2 ft. wide, while taking up about 6½ sq. ft. of floor space.

Make a long built-in manageable

The bookcase is only 1 ft. deep, but it's 10 ft. long. That posed some problems. I couldn't assemble and finish the project in place, and in my small shop, it wasn't practical to build the case as a single unit. So I divided it into two 5-ft.-long plywood boxes joined in the middle. Face frames on the front and back of the case, along with an MDF beadboard back, span the seam and give the case structural rigidity (see the drawings on pp. 152–153). The plywood cases are straightforward, assembled with #20 biscuits and 2-in. screws.

The only nonstandard detail is at the bottom of the bookcase, and it is something that normally would never be seen.

Because this bookcase cantilevers into the stairwell, a strip of the finish wood several inches wide had to be let into the bottom of the case.

Paint first, then assemble. Prime and paint interior surfaces before assembly. Use painter's tape to keep paint from clogging biscuit slots. Also, cut or drill holes for adjustable shelving.

Before assembling the boxes, I cut the holes for shelf pins, and with help from my wife, Susan, painted all interior surfaces. Painter's tape kept biscuit slots free of paint.

With the cases clamped together temporarily, I took all the measurements I needed for the face frames. Then I pushed the cases out of the way and got to work on the face frames.

Add interest with small, textured, decorative panels

Like the carcase, the face frames were built in sections. To join the boxes, the front and back of the case got a 6-ft.-wide face frame in the center. Then each end got a smaller face frame, roughly 2 ft. wide on the ends.

Cutting mortises and tenons is an antiquated approach in the era of the Kreg pocket-hole jig, but the joinery is reliable and strong. The wood is utile, a West African hardwood often used as a substitute for South American mahogany. It has some attractive ribbon stripping, machines well, and sands and finishes nicely.

(continued on p. 154)

A long cabinet with traditional joinery and improvised details replaces a traditional stairway railing.

Furniture-Grade Details from All Angles

OFFICE VIEW

Instead of a traditional railing, the author chose to enclose the open side of an office stairwell with a long bookcase. At 36 in. high, it meets code requirements, increases the room's storage capacity, and adds a new level of style. Cantilevered over the stairs, the bookcase occupies little floor space. A ledger and corbels provide decorative support.

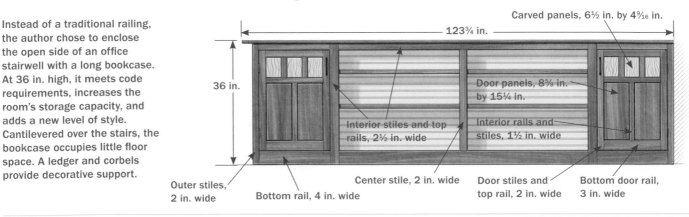

Carved panels, 6½ in. by 4⁹⁄₁₆ in.

123¾ in.

36 in.

Door panels, 8⅝ in. by 15¼ in.

Interior stiles and top rails, 2½ in. wide

Interior rails and stiles, 1½ in. wide

Outer stiles, 2 in. wide

Bottom rail, 4 in. wide

Center stile, 2 in. wide

Door stiles and top rail, 2 in. wide

Bottom door rail, 3 in. wide

STAIRWELL VIEW

Carved panels, 6⁷⁄₁₆ in. wide

Middle panels, 10³⁄₈ in. wide

Top overhang, 3 in.

Width of rails and stiles match those on the front.

Outer panels, 9³⁄₄ in. wide

Ledger and corbels

END VIEW

14 in.

Top overhang, 1 in.

End panel, 6½ in. wide

End stiles, 2 in. wide

35 ln.

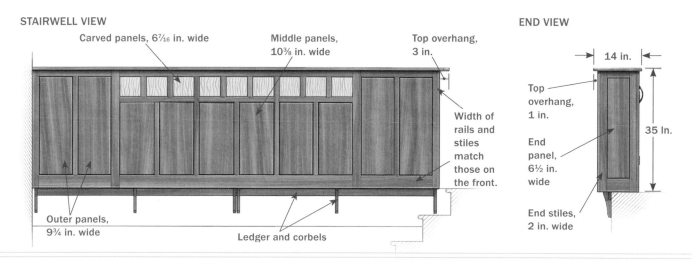

Face Frames Tie the Unit Together

Because of its 10-ft. length, the carcase was made from two 5-ft.-long halves joined at the center (1). The parts were assembled with screws, biscuits, and glue. The top stretchers were let into the sides for strength. Next, the three-piece beadboard back was attached (2), followed by front and back face frames, which were glued and clamped to the carcase (3-6). Any potential weakness where the two case halves are joined is compensated for by the overlay of the face frames.

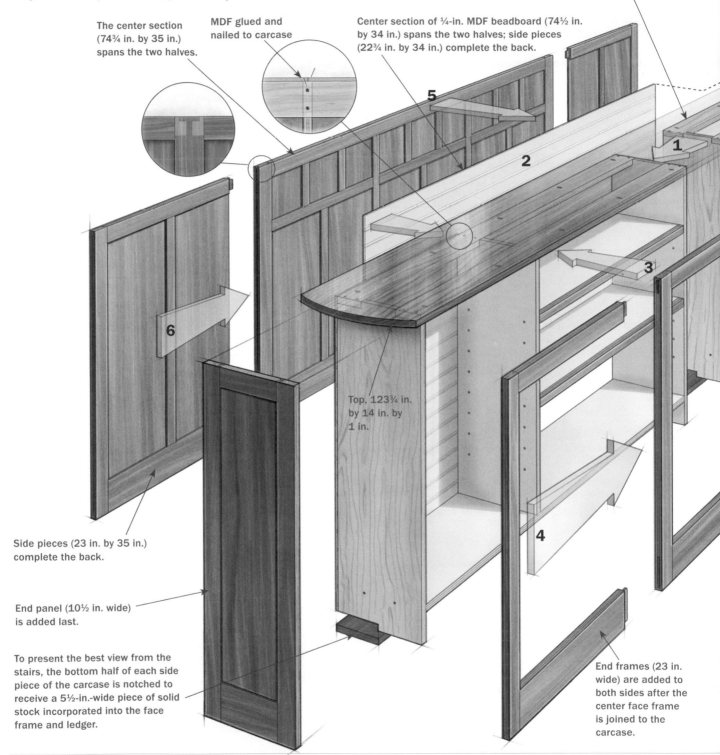

The center section (74¾ in. by 35 in.) spans the two halves.

MDF glued and nailed to carcase

Center section of ¼-in. MDF beadboard (74½ in. by 34 in.) spans the two halves; side pieces (22¾ in. by 34 in.) complete the back.

Two plywood boxes, each measuring 60 in. by 35 in. by 10¼ in.

Top, 123¾ in. by 14 in. by 1 in.

Side pieces (23 in. by 35 in.) complete the back.

End panel (10½ in. wide) is added last.

To present the best view from the stairs, the bottom half of each side piece of the carcase is notched to receive a 5½-in.-wide piece of solid stock incorporated into the face frame and ledger.

End frames (23 in. wide) are added to both sides after the center face frame is joined to the carcase.

Slotted screw holes in stretchers allow the top to move seasonally without cracking.

Shelf edging, 1 in. by ¾ in.

A 74¾-in. by 35-in. face frame joins the two halves of the carcase in front, spanning their common seam.

Doors with a whimsical variation

Mortise-and-tenon joints were used on the face frames and doors. The tenons were cut on a tablesaw, and the mortises were quickly excavated with a benchtop mortiser (see the photo below left). The haunched tenon adds strength and fills the exposed slot cut for panels.

The decorative panels were first cut, then secured between two stops. A router fitted with a ½-in. core-box bit was used to freehand the designs (see the photo below right). The panels were given two coats of paint before they were incorporated into the frames.

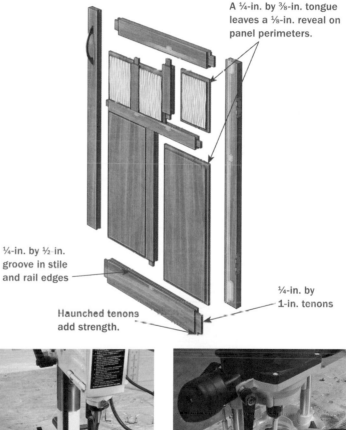

A ¼-in. by ⅜-in. tongue leaves a ⅛-in. reveal on panel perimeters.

¼-in. by ½-in. groove in stile and rail edges

¼-in. by 1-in. tenons

Haunched tenons add strength.

Make it quick. Cut the mortises with a benchtop mortiser.

You don't need a template. Freehand the decorative panels with a router.

To break up the monotony of all that utile on the section facing the stairwell, I introduced nine small panels, each about 6 in. square. I added texture to the face of each panel with the tip of a ½-in. core-box router bit, painted the panels the same color as the cabinet interior, and sanded them lightly to let some of the wood show through. I used the same panels to dress up the doors on the office-facing side of the bookcase.

Before gluing up the paneled section facing the stairs, I finished any edges that would be inaccessible. After the section was glued up, I pinned the panels in place from the back side with small nails, one nail in the middle of each panel top and bottom. The pins let the panels move with changes in humidity but keep them centered.

Glue-up is challenging

With the two big face-frame sections assembled and the rest of the parts and pieces milled, I was ready to give up the floor space in my shop and put the carcase together. I screwed together the two plywood boxes, tipped the case on its face, and attached the

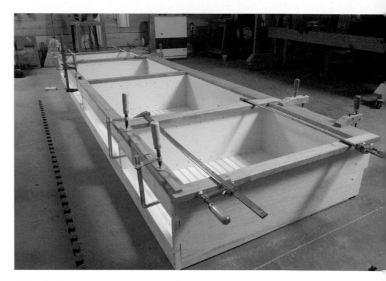

Attach the face frames one side at a time. The front face frame is attached first, then the back.

Strong and good-looking. Because a third of the width of the case is cantilevered over the stairwell, securing the cabinet in place was critical. A ledger supported by double corbels was screwed into the double LVL stair header.

center piece of MDF beadboard with glue and nails. Then I rolled the case on its back and glued on the first frame.

In advance, I'd milled mortises in the stiles on each end of the center frame so that the other pieces could be added in sections: first the 6-ft.-wide center section, then the wings on each side. Building the case this way meant I didn't have to handle or machine any pieces of lumber much longer than 75 in.

When the case had a complete front face frame, I repeated the process on the back: first the preassembled frame-and-panel center section, then the two end frames and their panels. Then I sanded down everything and finished it with a wipe-on polyurethane finish.

I left the doors and top for later to reduce the weight of the case, and with some borrowed muscle, I moved the case out of the shop, into the house, and then up the stairs.

Add brackets, and install the case

With only one-third of the case cantilevered over the stairwell, most of the bookcase's weight is supported by the floor. But to prevent the case from tipping, I installed a ledger and five corbels. The 1-in.-thick, 7½-in.-long corbels are notched, glued, and screwed to the ledger. The ledger is screwed to the face of the stairwell opening.

The bookcase abuts a wall at the far end of the stairwell, and here, I ran screws through the end and then into the wall framing to anchor it. To set the rest of the bookcase, I ran long screws through the bottom of the case into the floor; then I plugged the counterbores and touched up the paint.

When the rest of the rail system for the stairs is installed, I'll tie the bookcase to the post at the top of the stairs.

After the case was moved into position, 6-in. by ⁵⁄₁₆-in. screws were driven through the cabinet into the subflooring and, where possible, the framing. The end opposite the top of the stairs was screwed into the wall framing as well.

Space-Saving Scheme Needs Extra Support

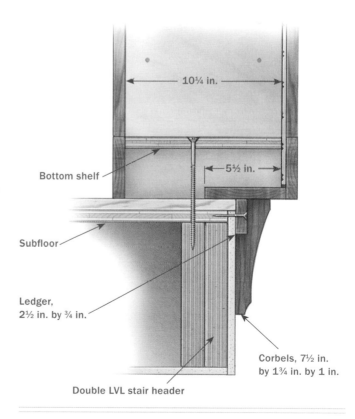

10¼ in.

Bottom shelf

5½ in.

Subfloor

Ledger, 2½ in. by ¾ in.

Corbels, 7½ in. by 1¾ in. by 1 in.

Double LVL stair header

Six Rules for Fast and Foolproof Cabinetmaking

SVEN HANSON

In my years as a cabinetmaker, I've found that it's rarely the big stroke of genius that makes the difference; rather, it's the avoidance of dumb mistakes. Simplifying cabinet designs and standardizing construction have made me feel a whole lot smarter. By making frameless cabinets, ordering the doors and drawer fronts from an outside vendor, and using production-oriented jigs, I've eliminated a lot of expensive router bits and stock preparation. Follow these guidelines, and you'll be able to go from shop drawings to finished cabinets quickly and accurately, with a minimal number of expensive tools and mistakes.

Rule 1: Build the boxes, but buy the doors

Making cabinet doors doubles the amount of time needed to build a kitchen, so I let someone else do it. Before I start building cabinets, I order doors and drawer fronts from an outside supplier. They're usually ready (including sanding and finishing, if specified) by the time I've built the cabinet cases. It's hard for me to meet the quality/price ratio that a shop delivers; two such

Efficient construction techniques can create beautiful results. A roomful of cabinets is easier to build with simple joinery, a few jigs, and some tactical advice.

suppliers are www.scherrs.com and www. lakesidemoulding.com.

Doors and drawer fronts can be ordered in any size and in a wide variety of styles. Factory-applied finishes are an option, but may be hard to match to cabinet boxes. Drawers and roll-out shelves make base cabinets more useful. With a drilling jig, drawer-slide hardware is easy to install. Use full-extension drawer slides. For sticky drawers, trim the drawer width where the slides attach by moving the drawer box through a tablesaw with the blade height set at about 2 in. Use concealed hinges for doors. They are complex-looking and more expensive than other types of hinges, but they're adjustable in three directions, making the doors easier to install.

Concealed hinges look complicated but make installation easier.

When building the cases, I simplify the joinery. Cabinet cases are made from ¾-in. veneered plywood. Assembly is done with glue and 1⅝-in. trim screws. Use ¼-in.

Simplified construction will maximize output and minimize mistakes.

plywood backs to square the cases. I use applied end panels. Any exposed screws in case sides will be hidden when the cabinets are joined together. For end-of-run cabinet sides, use finished plywood panels. In the base, the toe kick isn't part of the cabinet. Instead, I make case construction (and cabinet installation) easier by setting the cabinet box on a platform framed in 2x material.

Rule 2: Finish before you start

Edgebanding and applying a finish are best done to big pieces, but not too big. My usual strategy is to rip 4x8 sheets of plywood into 2x8 pieces, a size that's easy to finish and move. You'll have to go back and add a little edgebanding after all the parts are cut, but working on 2x8 sheets first will get the work done faster.

Using the plywood as a ruler, I snap off a bunch of 97-in.-long strips of edging. With the help of a spring clamp, I balance a strip on the top edge of the plywood sheet so that

Eliminate fixed shelves in base cabinets. You will have more usable space with drawers or roll-out shelves.

Iron on the edging. Secure one end first, then turn the iron toward the other end.

When you're ready to trim the edging, trim one edge at a time.

it overhangs each end. With the iron on a hot (linen) setting, I tack down one end of the edgeband, then iron toward the other end. To ensure good adhesion, scuff the plywood edge beforehand with 80-grit sandpaper, then clean the dust from the surface.

Edge trimmers normally trim both sides at once. That's fine for vinyl edging, but you'll get smoother results with wood if you show some respect for the grain. Pull the tool apart, and work one side at a time to avoid splits.

Before applying the varnish, it's a good idea to raise the grain with a damp sponge, then knock down the fuzzies with 220 grit sandpaper. This method speeds the process

Don't waste time finishing both sides. Pick the best-looking side and finish only that one.

When the varnish has dried, I knock down the bumps before applying a second coat. Sandpaper works fine, but I like to smooth the finish with a cabinet scraper.

Single-edge razor blades make great scrapers for the edgebanding.

by requiring fewer coats to get a finer finish. I like Parks Pro Finisher varnish (www. newparks.com). I finish the banded edge and one side (the better-looking one) of each piece, which then becomes the inside of the cabinet. If you finish both sides, you're mostly wasting time on surfaces that you'll cover up later with adjacent cabinets, drawers, or end panels. After assembly, I finish any visible outer surfaces.

Rule 3: Stick with basic dimensions

I begin the process by making a cutlist of all the parts I'll need (sides, tops, bottoms, backs, etc.) and note the dimensions both on the cutlist and on an unfinished end of the part (ballpoint ink will last). I use basic dimensions that divide well into a plywood panel. To account for the sawkerf, subtract ⅛ in. from the following sizes: 6 in. and 9 in. work well for drawers and toe-kick stock; 12 in., 16 in., and 18 in. work well for varying depths of upper-cabinet sides, tops, and bottoms; 24 in. is good for base cabinets.

Cut plywood efficiently. To avoid making crosscuts in full-size sheets of plywood, I rip sheets lengthwise, then turn to crosscutting. My shopmade crosscut sled rides in the tablesaw's miter-gauge slots, making precise crosscutting easy to do.

Rule 4: Speed assembly with simple joinery and a low table

I rarely rabbet cabinet backs or dado drawer bottoms. Instead, I fasten backs and bottoms directly to the edge of the plywood with polyurethane construction adhesive and nails or screws. When assembling, I use home-made corner blocks and a low assembly table to keep things square and at a comfortable working height.

Plywood cutoffs with square corners and lipped sides work well for clamping cabinet sides together or, as shown below left, for drawer assembly. I use a drawer side as a gauge to space the blocks properly. Then, with front and back standing, I wedge a side between them to keep them steady while fastening the other side.

With the drawer sides assembled, use the drawer bottoms to rack and hold the boxes square. I prefer plywood over hardboard or medium-density fiberboard for the bottoms (and cabinet backs) because of its light weight, durability, and ability to hold fasteners.

TIP Sand off the finish that will be glued. A rabbeted sanding block allows me to do this quickly and neatly. With a piece of 80-grit sand-paper glued in the rabbet, I rough up the varnished surface that receives the butt joint.

Corner blocks

Corner blocks are made with shop scraps. They can be used during cabinet or drawer assembly.

The bottom is structural. It will hold the box square as you assemble it.

Don't crawl into a cabinet to install drawer hardware. Do it on a bench instead.

Rule 5: Use drilling templates

Because I think that base cabinets with fixed shelves are a sin against common sense, I fill them with drawers or roll-out upgrades. But installing all that drawer hardware can be finicky business. I avoid a lot of mistakes by using a full-size template made from ¼-in. plywood or melamine. My template defines the positions of the holes for drawer slides in kitchen base cabinets (three- and four-drawer type), vanity cabinets, and file drawers, too. I simply color-code the holes to minimize mistakes.

With the cabinet on its side and the template wedged in place, I drill the holes for the drawer slides with a cordless drill (see the top photo on the facing page). Flip over the cabinet and template, align the front edge, and drill holes in the other side.

For upper cabinets with adjustable shelves, I ensure accurate hole spacing by using a drilling template, which I made with a piece of melamine on a friend's line-boring

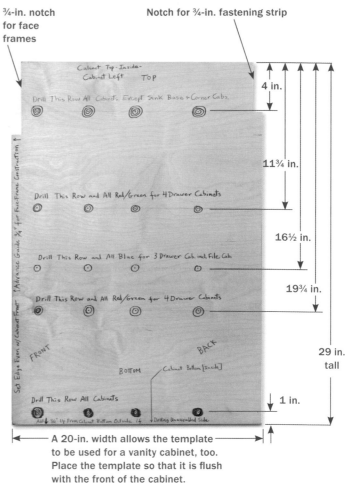

A 20-in. width allows the template to be used for a vanity cabinet, too. Place the template so that it is flush with the front of the cabinet.

machine. You also can buy a template from most woodworking stores. This template's spacing ensures consistency and lets you take advantage of the European cabinetmaking system, with holes every 16 mm (⅝ in.) that align shelves and hardware. Set this template against the bottom of the cabinet, and work your way up. The template is symmetrical, but working from the bottom up avoids any problems caused by a cabinet side that may have been cut a bit shorter than the other.

With the shelf template, use a cordless drill to place shelf holes accurately.

1⁷⁄₁₆ in.

2½ in.

1¼ in.

Off-center holes allow the template to be used for frameless or face-frame cabinets.

TIP Install the cabinet backs last after drilling holes and installing the hardware. This approach boosts your screw-driving comfort zone by allowing access from front or back.

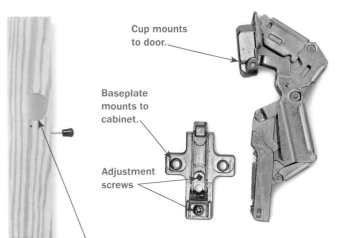

Cup mounts to door.

Baseplate mounts to cabinet.

Adjustment screws

The cup hole must be close to the edge of the door, or the door will rub against the cabinet when opened and closed. You almost can't be too close, but you certainly can be too far. About ⅛ in. will allow the door to overlay the cabinet frame fully without rubbing. With the cup hinge squarely in the hole, set one screw. This will ensure that all hinges are installed consistently.

Set the adjustable bumpers after the first set of hinges is in place and working well.

Drill holes all the way through so that the stick can be used for left- or right-hinging and as a drilling guide.

Cup holes are drilled an equal distance from the end so that the stick can be flipped top or bottom.

Rule 6: Install doors with a hinge stick

European-style hinges come in two pieces: a cup and a baseplate. The cup mounts to the door, and the baseplate mounts to the cabinet side. The two parts then snap or screw together. Because they're two-part hinges, it's crucial that the corresponding pieces line up, or they won't snap together. My hinge stick keeps the distance between baseplates and the setback from cabinet front consistent. To use it, insert cup hinges into the holes, and with hinges in the closed position, screw the baseplates to the cabinet side. Test the operation of the hinge stick. If all's well, adjust the bumpered screws to the distance between the open door and the cabinet. Now you can install all the baseplates with the stick in the open position.

Shelf-pin holes

Align the hinge stick with the top of the cabinet, drill pilot holes, and drive the baseplate screws. The bumpers ensure consistent setback on all the hinges.

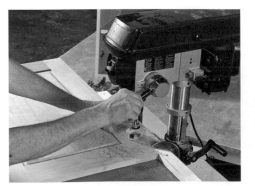

The best way to bore the cup holes is to use a 1⅜-in. Forstner bit with a depth stop in a benchtop drill press. Set up a fence with reference marks to ensure consistent alignment (see the photo at far left). Without a benchtop drill press, the hinge stick can make a good drilling template if clamped to the door.

A Faster, Easier Approach to Custom Cabinets

MIKE MAINES

When designed and constructed properly, built-in cabinets can bring both style and storage to many parts of a home. Over the years, I've refined my approach to constructing cabinets to decrease the time and tools it takes to build them while ensuring their strength and good looks. I used my technique to build the Douglas-fir kitchen island featured here for my home, but I've followed the same process to make stain- and paint-grade kitchen cabinets, bookcases, linen cabinets, pantries, desks, bathroom vanities, and storage cubbies.

Your shop is where you make it

The beauty of this system is that the setup is simple and doesn't rely on the space or tools found in big cabinet shops. Being able to set up shop in a driveway, a garage, or a small room has always been helpful in keeping my work on schedule.

There are several specific tools that will help the work progress smoothly. For cutting components to size, you need a miter saw, a portable tablesaw, a circular saw, an edge guide to cut sheet goods safely, and a portable thickness planer. To fasten the carcase and face frames together, you need a 16-ga. or 18-ga. finish nailer, a screw gun, a pocket-screw jig (www.kregtool.com; www.pennstateind.com), a bunch of screws, and some glue.

A hybrid design makes face-frame cabinets better

Cabinets are typically designed in one of two ways: frameless or with face frames. Each has its merits. Face-frame cabinets are traditional and strong, and they can be scribed to fit seamlessly against a wall. Frameless cabinets are quicker to put together and can be used in conjunction with adjustable, hidden, and now soft-close hinges.

I've done a lot of historically informed work, and frameless boxes just don't provide the appeal of face-frame cabinets with inset doors. Although frameless cabinets allow a bit more space inside, their end panels tend to look tacked-on, crown molding is hard to detail properly, and filler strips are heavily relied on during installation. I use the benefits of both styles by building a hybrid cabinet. Flushing the inside of the carcase to the inside of the face frame allows me to use hardware designed for frameless cabinets while still providing the traditional look, ease of installation, and strength of face-frame construction.

TIP A face frame can be nailed to a box with 16-ga. finish nails. However, the holes still need to be filled, and the gun can scuff the face-frame surface. Another way to attach face frames is with biscuit joinery, which is a solid solution but one that demands a lot of time and a massive arsenal of clamps. By attaching the face frame with pocket screws, I get an immediate, permanent connection while leaving the face of the cabinet clear.

Good proportions are no accident

Although my built-in cabinets are assembled easily, there's no guarantee they'll look good in a home. A cabinet constructed with wacky proportions won't look or function as well as it should. To start, make a scale drawing on paper of each piece you intend to build. Having this reference on hand will give you a clear idea of what you're building and help you to create a detailed cutlist. I follow a few basic rules when it comes to designing cabinets.

- Built-in cabinets that will be used as workstations generally have countertops 36 in. above the floor, so boxes should be built to a height of 34½ in. to 35 in., depending on the thickness of the countertop. Cabinets that aren't task-oriented can be any size and are built without toe kicks. I distinguish these units by building the bottom rail taller or shorter than the house's baseboard. When in doubt of any proportions, I use the golden rectangle, a shape 1.6 times as high as it is wide. I also find the widths of components by dividing similar members by 1.6 as done with the end-panel rails.

- When multiple cabinet boxes are lined up in a row, they appear more fitted when tied together with a single face frame. I connect the boxes by hiding a screw behind each door hinge. You can make all the face-frame components the same size, but that can make the rails look fat and the end stiles look skinny. Instead, I like to adjust their widths (see the drawing on the facing page) so that the built-in looks more balanced.

- Doors always should be taller than they are wide and never should exceed 20 in. in width; otherwise they project too far into a space when opened. Even an 18-in.-wide door can be too large on certain units. Drawers should be left with a flat face when they're shorter than 4½ in., which is typical, and can be detailed to match frame-and-panel doors when they're taller.

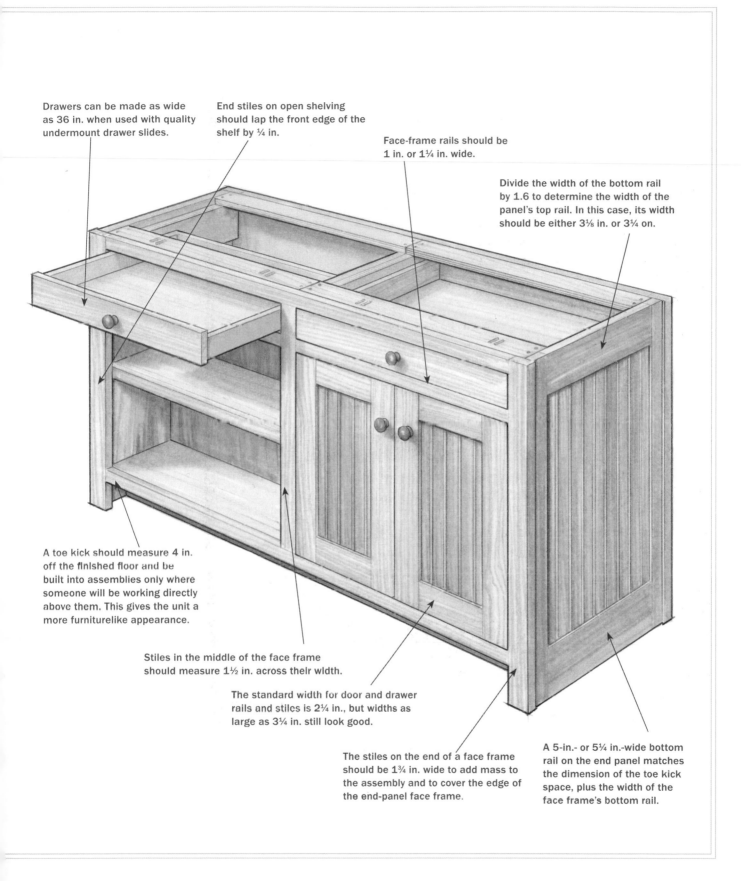

Drawers can be made as wide as 36 in. when used with quality undermount drawer slides.

End stiles on open shelving should lap the front edge of the shelf by ¼ in.

Face-frame rails should be 1 in. or 1¼ in. wide.

Divide the width of the bottom rail by 1.6 to determine the width of the panel's top rail. In this case, its width should be either 3⅛ in. or 3¼ on.

A toe kick should measure 4 in. off the finished floor and be built into assemblies only where someone will be working directly above them. This gives the unit a more furniturelike appearance.

Stiles in the middle of the face frame should measure 1½ in. across their width.

The standard width for door and drawer rails and stiles is 2¼ in., but widths as large as 3¼ in. still look good.

The stiles on the end of a face frame should be 1¾ in. wide to add mass to the assembly and to cover the edge of the end-panel face frame.

A 5-in.- or 5¼ in.-wide bottom rail on the end panel matches the dimension of the toe kick space, plus the width of the face frame's bottom rail.

Rip stock to width. Use a tablesaw to square all boards with rounded edges. Then cut all face-frame components ⅛ in. wider than their final dimension.

Plane similar parts together. Instead of planing each board individually, plane to their exact width all the endstiles, then inner stiles, then rails.

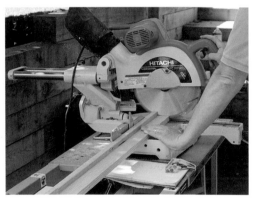

Chop to length. Armed with a fence and a stop made of scrap material, and a cutlist, chop all the face-frame material to its precise length. Stack all the material to make a complete face frame.

Building the cabinets

When milling 1x6 face-frame material to size, I like to fine-tune its final width with a planer, not a tablesaw. I rip the face-frame stock ⅛ in. wider than I need on a tablesaw. Then I remove the last ⅛ in. with a planer (see the top right photo). The planer produces more precise dimensions and smoother cuts.

I build all the face frames before I build their corresponding boxes (see the photos on the facing page). This not only saves room on the job site, but it also allows me to use

Lay out the parts, and mark pocket-hole locations. Dry-fit the face-frame components so that their grain and color look best. Mark the boards to show their orientation in the assembly and the place where they'll be pocket-screwed.

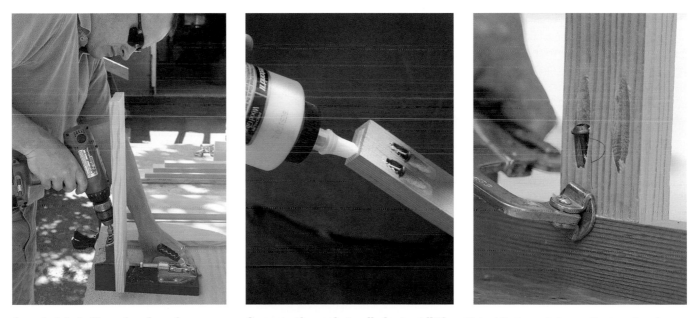

A pocket-hole jig makes face-frame assembly easy. Drill two pocket holes in the end of each rail and each inner stile.

Squeeze the grain to eliminate splitting. Put a bit of wood glue on the board end before securing a locking C-clamp so that it exerts equal pressure on the grain of each component. The clamp should be placed in line with the pocket hole being screwed.

Quality control. Check to be sure that every component is aligned and secured properly before building subsequent frames. Accuracy here is crucial because the dimensions of the face frame might be used as a reference when building the boxes.

the face frames for reference when a dimension comes into question during carcase construction.

Box assembly is a relatively straightforward process (see the photos on the facing page). Before the sides of the boxes are fastened together, though, I drill pocket holes and the holes for shelving pins. I drill two pocket holes because, while the face frame should flush with the inside of the box perfectly, if it doesn't, having multiple holes gives me the flexibility to push and pull the face frame into alignment.

Screws, glue, and quality hardware hold it together

Traditionally, face-frame cabinets are constructed with dadoes, grooves, dowels, or mortise-and-tenon joinery to lock together each component. These techniques create strong assemblies, too, but require much more time.

I assemble face frames with fine-thread, 1¼-in. square-drive washer-head pocket screws and yellow glue (see the bottom photos on p. 169). I tack the carcases together with finish nails and then drive 1⅝-in. drywall screws for strength. I've used drywall screws for years and have never had a cabinet fail, but it's important to use stronger screws when attaching a cabinet to the wall.

Beyond box strength, cabinets often are measured by the quality of their hardware.

TIP I make a simple jig out of thin MDF to orient shelf pinholes 1½ in. from the front and back of the box. I usually place the first hole 12 in. off the bottom of the box and drill holes in 1½-in. increments above and below.

Cut sheet goods safely. Full sheets of plywood should never be cut on a table saw. Instead, use a straightedge clamped to the sheet's surface and a circular saw with a fine-toothed alternate top bevel (ATB) sawblade.

Drill pocket holes for the boxes in groups of two. When preparing the sides of the carcase that will be joined with the face frame, drill two holes instead of one for each connection point. This extra step will come in handy when attaching the face frames.

Tack and screw together the box parts. Nailing the box with 16-ga. finish nails makes it easier to keep pieces in place while they're locked together with 1⅝-in. drywall screws.

Support the box and the drawer slides. On top of each box and below each drawer, ¾-in. plywood crosspieces add strength, a place to connect the face frame's top rail, and a surface to attach countertops and undermount drawer slides.

Attach the face frame to the boxes with pocket screws.

The best hinge for this hybrid system is a 32-mm cup hinge made by Blum (www. blum.com) or Grass® (www.grassusa.com). Adjustable, self-closing, and quick to install, they are usually my first choice. In more historically accurate work where a visible hinge is preferred or when I don't want a hinge to intrude on storage space, I like to use Cliffside's 2-in. butt hinges (www. cliffsideind.com). I use a trim router to mortise the door for a single leaf and don't

The face frame should flush with the inside of the box perfectly, but if it doesn't, having mulitiple holes gives you the flexibility to push and pull the face frame into alignment.

Dress up an exposed end panel

Built-in cabinets usually have their sides buried in a wall. Sometimes, however, the sides and even the back are exposed to public view. I detail these areas to hide pocket holes in a couple of ways.

On my kitchen island, I'm using a stock of reclaimed Douglas-fir edge and center bead that has been collecting dust in my garage for years. I simply fill the face-frame opening with the boards, attaching them with an 18-ga. pin nailer. Held tight against the carcase, the ¾-in.-thick face frame would leave a ¼-in. reveal where it meets the end stiles of the front face frame. So I fur out the end panel with ³⁄₁₆-in. plywood strips to reduce the size of the reveal.

If I'm not going to use beadboard on a built-in, I fill the face frame with ½-in. plywood to create a flat recessed panel. Alternatively, I cover the entire side of the carcase with a sheet of ¼-in. plywood that can be stained or painted to match the wood I've used, then I glue and nail the face frame to it.

Cover your tracks. To hide pocket holes and screws used to assemble the cabinet, wrap exposed faces with a decorative material, such as stain- or paint-grade plywood, beadboard, or edge and center bead.

mortise the face frame at all, which helps to provide just the right reveal between the door and the face frame.

I've used all three types of drawer slides in my cabinets, but when I have a choice, I opt for the Blum Tandem®, an undermount full-extension unit that is forgiving to install and smooth to operate.

For adjustable shelves, I like to drill groups of three to five holes where I think the shelf should be. This allows some adjustability while avoiding the factory-made look of a continuous row of holes. Often, I use paddle-type supports installed in a 5-mm hole. For heavy-duty applications, such as a bookshelf, I like an L-shaped pin in a ¼-in. hole.

Get doors and drawer fronts that fit the second time

I order or build doors and drawer fronts before the cabinet boxes are complete so that I can finish the job quickly. To be sure they fit the way I want them to, with the perfect reveal, I order or build them to the exact size of the face-frame opening written on my plans. Once on site, I fit them tight into their openings. I reduce their size on all sides a heavy ¹⁄₁₆ in. by taking measurements from the face frame, not the door or drawer front itself, and ripping them on the tablesaw.

Four Quick Cabinet Upgrades

GARY STRIEGLER

Kitchen remodels are a priority for many of my clients, but some budgets won't allow you to gut the kitchen and install all new cabinets, fixtures, and appliances. So I've developed methods to give improved function and a style upgrade without breaking the bank, and you don't have to be a contractor to pull these off. The concept is simple: Give the existing cabinets an overhaul. By adding new doors and drawers, upgrading storage, dressing things up with trim, and then applying a glazed paint job, I can tie the new components in with the old ones for a seamless face-lift. Upgrading the cabinets took me six days and cost about $600 in materials. The backsplash cost about $225 and took another day to install. I hired out the granite countertop and the painting.

There are a couple of prerequisites. First, the cabinet boxes need to be in sound condition. Adding new doors and drawers to poorly constructed boxes makes about as much sense as building a new house on a crumbling foundation. Second, the existing materials and style of construction are a big factor. The kitchen shown here had site-built face-frame cabinets made with a combination of solid wood and plywood, common in older houses. If the cabinets had been made from particleboard or didn't have face frames, the process would have been more complicated, and the return on investment less promising.

Dark and dated cabinets (above) were renewed, creating a brand-new look (see facing page) for less money.

Solid doors become framed panels

On this project, the existing cabinet doors were made from ¾-in. mahogany plywood. The plywood was in decent condition, so I wanted to find a way to reuse it. Most flat-panel cabinet doors tend to be made with ¼-in.- to ½-in.-thick plywood panels, which are lightweight and inexpensive but also feel cheap in terms of quality. I decided to use the old doors as panels, setting each in a new frame to create a more substantial cabinet door. If I hadn't been able to use the doors for the new panels, I would likely have

After the door-frame stock is cut to width and rabbeted to receive the panel, rout the other edge with a ⅜-in. beading bit.

chosen MDF, which is extremely stable and takes paint well.

For the door-frame stock, I chose poplar, a relatively inexpensive closed-grain hardwood that looks excellent in paint-grade cabinetry. Other hardwoods like maple and oak are good choices for stain-grade door frames as well. In terms of cost and durability, though, poplar can't be beat. The door construction is simple. It's crucial, however, that all of the wood be milled, that the rabbets be cut, and that beaded profiles be routed before the stock is cut to final size, or the cuts may not match up properly.

A pair of pocket screws at each miter creates a tight joint. The holes then are plugged and sanded flush.

A hinge-boring jig (www.eurolimited.com) makes quick work of preparing each door to receive the new concealed hinges.

Cut the old doors down to become panels, and cut a matching rabbet around each so that it will sit about ¼ in. below the front face of the frame.

The panel molding, which also gets a shallow rabbet before assembly, is used to secure the panel in place and hide the joint.

New drawers in an hour

The existing drawers in this kitchen were made from 1x pine and assembled with glued rabbet joints reinforced with nails. Decades of use had loosened the drawer boxes and left the aluminum drawer slides sticky or falling apart.

This kitchen (and its budget) didn't warrant a high-end drawer with dovetail joints and hidden self-closing drawer slides. Instead, I built the drawers in this project from birch plywood. They are just as strong as the boxes found in high-end kitchen cabinets, and each takes me less than an hour to complete.

The construction of each drawer—butt joints, pocket screws, and a bottom panel captured in a dado—is simple. Installation is a bit more complicated, however, because site-built cabinets don't typically have back panels, so a plywood backer is needed for solid attachment of the drawer slides.

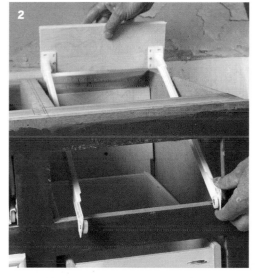

After cutting a backerboard equal to the interior width of each cabinet, use the face frame as a template to mark the drawer-slide mounts before nailing the panel into place at the back of each cabinet.

Attach the brackets and drawer slides to a plywood cleat, and install each preassembled unit as one piece.

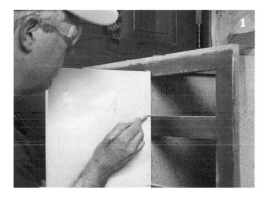

Slide the drawer box into place, and use a straightedge to adjust the slides until the drawer box is flush with the face frame. Then drive the screws to secure the assembly.

Using a spacer jig to establish a consistent height above the cabinet doors, secure each drawer front from the inside of the drawer box with screws.

Doors and larger drawer fronts are routed with the bead profile before the stock is cut to length and assembled. Smaller drawer fronts can be made from solid poplar dressed up with a mitered bead detail installed separately using glue and pin nails.

1

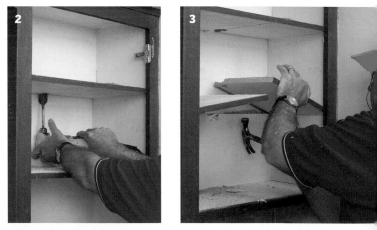

2

3

To remove the old shelves, drill a hole in the rear center of the board (above left), then cut up to the hole with a jigsaw so that the shelf can be removed in two pieces (above right).

You can make your own shelf-pin drilling template, but a self-centering bit and a compatible drilling guide (www.eurolimited. com) make the job go much faster.

Fixed shelves become adjustable

Site-built cabinets typically have shelves set into dadoes, so they can't be moved up or down to accommodate items of different sizes. I like to rip out these old fixed shelves and then install new painted side panels that cover the dadoes and allow for adjustable shelving (see the bottom left photo).

Trim takes it from plain to pretty

If I were building cabinets from scratch, I would install the boxes and add the molding on site. An old kitchen isn't much different because what you have is a bunch of plain boxes ready for molding.

Old-style cabinets were typically designed for utility, not so much for elegance. The addition of molding helps to balance the look of the new doors and drawer fronts, adds depth and shadowlines, and most important, gussies up the whole installation. For a job like this, I typically add band molding at the bottom (see the photo below), crown molding at the top. Depending on the space remaining below the cabinet doors, another nailer may be necessary to provide solid backing for the band molding. Some extra blocking may be necessary at the top, too. On this job, I added a valance to provide solid nailing for part of the crown molding. If the cabinets don't extend to the ceiling, a nailer may be necessary at the top edge of the cabinet as well. I also add picture-frame molding wherever end panels will show (see the bottom right photo).

Band molding at the bottom dresses up the cabinet faces.

Insert the new side panel into place over the old inside of the cabinet, and secure it with finish nails.

The best approach for end panels is to preassemble the picture-frame molding and install it as one piece. Use spacers to center the molding, and then attach it using nails that won't penetrate into the cabinet interior.

Cabinet Door Shoot-Out

SCOTT GIBSON AND JOSEPH LANZA

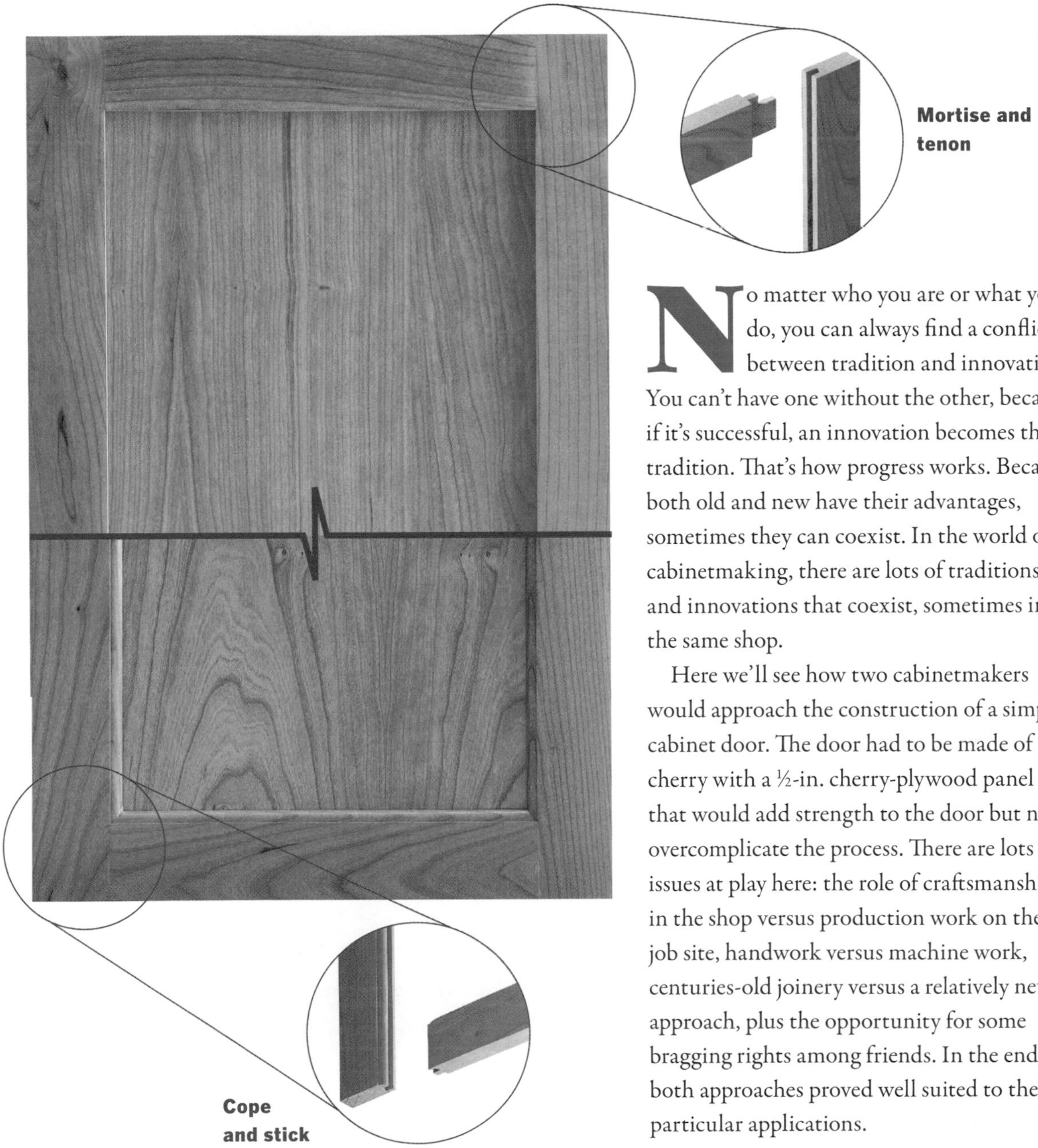

Mortise and tenon

Cope and stick

No matter who you are or what you do, you can always find a conflict between tradition and innovation. You can't have one without the other, because if it's successful, an innovation becomes the tradition. That's how progress works. Because both old and new have their advantages, sometimes they can coexist. In the world of cabinetmaking, there are lots of traditions and innovations that coexist, sometimes in the same shop.

Here we'll see how two cabinetmakers would approach the construction of a simple cabinet door. The door had to be made of cherry with a ½-in. cherry-plywood panel that would add strength to the door but not overcomplicate the process. There are lots of issues at play here: the role of craftsmanship in the shop versus production work on the job site, handwork versus machine work, centuries-old joinery versus a relatively new approach, plus the opportunity for some bragging rights among friends. In the end, both approaches proved well suited to their particular applications.

Mortises and tenons take more work initially, but once your setup is done you can work quickly.

Cope-and-stick doors are strong.

Mortise and tenon

BY SCOTT GIBSON

I have a lot of confidence in a traditional mortise-and-tenon door. The wood-to-wood contact is substantial, meaning there's a large glue area, and the joints are highly resistant to racking. A door with right-fitting joints is extremely durable.

The process is more time-consuming than making cope-and-stick joints with a router, and it isn't as well suited to making doors on a job site. That said, the work goes surprisingly fast once the machine settings have been dialed in. For tooling, I use a tablesaw and a mortising machine in addition to a few basic hand tools. Mortises could be cut with a drill press or even a portable drill plus a chisel, but the mortising machine is faster and more accurate.

It may be overkill to make doors the way I do, but it wouldn't be the first time I over-built something. The advantage I see is that with one setup, mortise-and-tenon joinery can be used to make all the frame-and-panel parts, face frames, and doors for a kitchen's worth of cabinets. It takes some fiddling to get the setup, but once that's done, many pieces can be run off quickly.

Cope and stick

BY JOSEPH LANZA

I don't know if it qualifies yet as traditional, but millwork factories were producing cope-and-stick joinery a hundred years ago. If you have a table-mounted router, cope-and-stick bits offer a quick, accurate way to make cabinet doors without a big investment.

With a glued-in plywood panel, cope-and-stick doors are extremely strong. Solid-panel doors can be made stronger by adding interior rails or stiles, but for larger doors, cope and stick may not be the best choice, unless the joints are reinforced with slip tenons or dowels. The extra work required might tip me in favor of using mortises and tenons for larger doors.

Although maybe not the best choice for period reproductions, cope-and-stick doors are a good option for jobs that don't require the structural or emotional benefits of mortise-and-tenon joinery. Most of the modern solid-wood cabinet doors in this country are made with a simple cope-and-stick joint, and the vast majority are holding up just fine.

Set up

Make a test piece first for setup. The one fixed dimension of the mortise and tenon is determined by the size of the mortiser chisel, so the tenon and panel groove are sized to the mortise. A test mortise is cut with a benchtop mortiser fitted with a ¼-in. bit (1). Measuring the width of the mortise with a set of dial calipers is an accurate way to determine the necessary thickness of the tenon and the panel groove (2).

Prep stiles and rails

Although the panel groove is often cut with a dado stack, it also can be cut with a single tablesaw blade. Because the groove measures ¼ in. wide, it can be cut by positioning the fence so that the blade cuts just to one side of the centerline. Registered from either side of the stock, the blade cuts a centered groove in two passes (1). After the panel groove is cut, the mortiser is set up to cut the mortises in the stiles on center and to the correct depth. Here, the mortises were cut to ¹⁵⁄₁₆ in. deep to make room for glue and a 1 ¼-in.-long tenon (2).

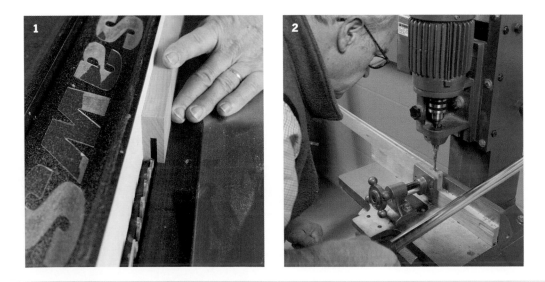

Cope and stick (continued)

Set up

Cope-and-stick router bits are available as single arbors with interchangeable cutters or in sets of dedicated cope and stick bits (1). The two-bit sets are more accurate and take much less time to set up. (The Amana Tool® set used here also can be used to make interior passage doors.) Many sets include thin brass or steel shims that can be inserted between the cutters to match the relative size of the profile to the thickness of the stock (2).

Cope end rails

Cut the cope first to reduce tearout. After chucking the cope bit into the router, adjust the bit height so that the profile is centered in the stock, and check with a test piece. The opening in the fence should be just large enough to allow the bit to spin without hitting the fence (1). With a straightedge, check that the bearing is in line with the fence. When cutting, use a backing block to keep the stock square to the bit and to prevent the grain from blowing out at the back of the piece (2). Cope all rail ends.

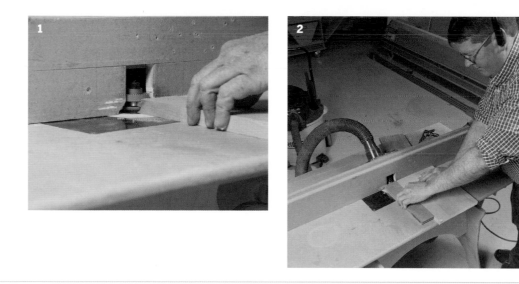

Tenon the rails

Using either a single blade or a dado stack, cut tenons by first registering the fence at a distance from the blade equal to the length of the tenon. The first pass will cut the cheeks, so it's important that the miter gauge be square to the blade. Moving the stock away from the fence and making repeated passes removes the waste (1). It's a good idea to check the setup on scrap first. Cut the tenon to width (2, 3). Each joint should be tested to ensure a tight fit before assembly (4). It's best if the tenon needs a few swipes with a plane to fit, rather than having to add a shim (5).

Stick the stiles and rails

Switch to the stick bit. After switching bits, align the middle cutter with the stub tenon on the coped end (1). Run a test piece to make sure the mating cope and stick align. Run all rails and stiles (2).

Rabbet the panel

Once the frame is ready to be assembled, the panel can be cut. In this case, ½-in. plywood was chosen for a more substantial door. After the panel was cut to size, a rabbet was routed along its back edge (1, 2).

Assemble the door

The last step is assembly. After a thin, even coat of glue is spread on the mating parts, the rails and one stile are joined. Next, the panel is inserted into the groove (1), the second stile is attached, and the door is clamped. Measure diagonals to make sure the door stays square in the clamps (2).

Cope and stick (continued)

Rabbet the panel

Dry-fit the rails and stiles (1), then determine the panel size. Because plywood won't move seasonally, the panel can be cut within ¹⁄₁₆ in. of the actual size. Set up the router table with a straight or dado bit to cut the ¼-in. by ½-in. rabbet on the panel's back (2).

Assemble the door

It's always a good idea to have a dry run when gluing up a door (1). If everything fits tightly, apply glue and assemble the rails, stiles, and panel. Clamp at both ends near the rails, and check that the door isn't curling because of too much clamp pressure. Parts that slide out of alignment under pressure can be adjusted back into place with a dead-blow mallet (2). Finally, check the diagonals to make sure the door is square (3).

Signature Details for Kitchen Cabinets

CHARLES BICKFORD

Depending on your point of view, the devil or deity of your choice is in the details, especially when it comes to cabinetry. After all, cabinets are essentially boxes to store stuff; the right details can raise the boxes to a higher function and aesthetic. The best details make a kitchen or pantry less like a collection of boxes and more like a piece of furniture, valued for its beauty as well as its function.

Subtle details make a difference—a slight curve on a lower rail or a softened edge where your fingers grab a door. But not all details are things you have to put your hands on to appreciate. A good detail can just as easily be a clever way to incorporate cabinets into the room; you might not appreciate the design until you stand back to look.

Like most things these days, cabinets are usually factory-made, and options for wood species, size, finish, and style are dizzyingly diverse. However, just because you have a choice doesn't necessarily mean it's the right choice. And that's where small shops come into the picture. Under the auspices of a smart designer, a small shop has the flexibility to transform the usual details of doors, drawers, face frames, and end panels into a kitchen or built-in as unique as the owner's face.

For the examples here, I tried to get an even distribution of regional work and styles, but I know I'm just scratching the surface.

Make the Appliances Go Away

Modern appliances, especially refrigerators, tend to overwhelm the scale of a kitchen. Cabinetmaker Jon Frost likes to push them back into a recess framed into a wall so that the visible portion is reduced.

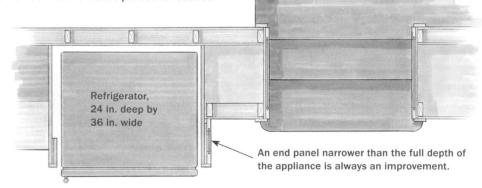

Refrigerator, 24 in. deep by 36 in. wide

An end panel narrower than the full depth of the appliance is always an improvement.

Freshen up your cabinets. A small shop can create truly custom details like these cabinets that help camouflage a large refrigerator.

Columns warm the color scheme. Basing the design on a profile taken from architect Edwin Lundie, who remodeled this particular house 70 years ago, Jon's shop turned a clear-finished quarter column of mahogany to punctuate the transition between an end panel and an adjacent built-in seat.

Fitting in. Double wall ovens blend into a wall of cabinets and display shelves.

Getting creative within the realm of tradition

Jon Frost lives and works in the Minneapolis area, which has a strong architectural tradition based in the late-Victorian period. He's been building cabinetry for the past 25 years, so it's no accident that Jon has mastered the traditional frame-and-panel style and has made his new work fit seamlessly into older houses, even as every year brings bigger and bigger modern appliances. "The Sub-Zeros® are too tall and bulky, in my opinion. ... We build the walls out to flank the fridge and oven units so that the cabinets don't look so large. We do that anywhere and everywhere we can." In one kitchen (see the photo on p. 189), the fridge appears to be about 9 in. proud of the wall; the rest is tucked back alongside the cased opening (see the drawing on p. 188). Sometimes Jon even covers the condenser panel with upper doors to bring the unit into scale.

He employed a similar trick to reduce the mass of a double wall oven (see the photo above left). This time, he also radiused the end display shelves. This is a busy, informal household, and the eased corners of this big unit keep traffic incidents to a minimum.

Getting more from less

Trained as an architect, **Joe Lanza** is also a builder and cabinetmaker in Duxbury, Massachusetts. Soon after moving into his house, he built his own cabinets from Baltic-birch plywood, which he likes to use without edgebanding.

Rather than run the cabinets straight across and lose space under the shed roof, he stepped them up for maximum storage space. Exposed washer-head lath screws on the end panels are there, as he put it, "for a bit of quasi-industrial neo-modernist anti-ornamental ornament." He used pneumatic nails where they wouldn't show. The door frames are solid birch with frosted-glass panels.

To reduce dead space above the cabinets on the lower slope, Joe used triangular MDF panels above the cabinets; he set them back ½ in. from the face of the cabinet boxes.

Upsetting the status quo with small details

A cabinetmaker and designer in the Seattle area, **David Getts** has found that his real forte is making things look deceptively simple. His bamboo-plywood kitchen (see the photos at right) is spare and sleek; the

Don't waste space. Following the line of the shed roof means maximum storage space from cabinets.

The material speaks for itself. Applied over stock cabinets, the bamboo plywood's laminations (above left) create a decorative edge that doesn't need edgebanding. The base cabinet's end panel (above right) is highlighted by a narrow kerf cut where the panel meets the unbanded edge of the front panel.

continuous grain pattern that runs from one side to the other is the big clue to his abilities. Look closer, and you see another important detail: Every door and drawer front is an unadorned piece of plywood, and the panels seem to be cut with a laser. The reveals are sharp and precise. David says that the material is easy to use and forgiving; he used a 60-tooth ATB blade in his tablesaw for all the cuts and cleaned everything up on a stationary belt sander.

David also uses a wide variety of materials to make his work distinctive. On an entertainment center's vertical-grain Douglas-fir doors (see the photo at right), he mixed smoked-glass panels and two sets of Häfele® pulls as an effective way of catching the eye. The pulls' brushed finish goes well with the warmth of the fir, which David favors for many of his projects.

On another set of doors, he used ¼-in. MDF panels (see the photo below) that

Grab the eye. Smoked glass and elegant hardware attract attention but aren't overdone.

seem to float inside the door frames. It's an uncluttered look that's inexpensive, and as he says, "You can use almost any ¼-in. material." In this instance, the panels were originally slated for a geometric design, but in the end were painted a solid color.

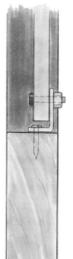

Expose your inner hardware. The hardware used to mount the panels onto the door frames is simple right-angle brackets from Häfele (www.hafele. com). The beauty of the design is that almost any material can be mounted without splitting or delaminating.

A Stickley-inspired island feels like a piece of furniture.

A new island inspired by an old piece of furniture

Rex Alexander of Brethren, Michigan, designed an island as the last part of a quartersawn red-oak kitchen he built (see the photo above). The homeowners needed a large stovetop cooking area, plenty of drawer space for pots and pans, and a place where the kids could do homework while watching their mother cook. His intention was to design something that looked more like a Gustav Stickley-inspired library table to serve as the family workstation. A 5-in.-tall by 9-in.-deep granite-topped divider helps to keep cooking spatters contained on the cooktop side.

To reduce costs, Rex built the interior casework from melamine, then applied the end panels, face frames, drawers, and doors.

The island was assembled on site; after installing a toe-kick box, he followed with individual cabinets, end panels, and a solid top of quartersawn oak. To fabricate the corner posts, Rex borrowed a building trick from Stickley, assembling each post from four quartersawn pieces with mitered edges. Assembled with biscuit joints and glue, the posts are dimensionally stable and show off perfect edge grain on all sides.

A woven pantry door pulls out like a drawer

The ventilated door panel is an idea that has been used for years on boat interiors. Caned like a chair seat or woven like a basket, the lightweight door panels allow air to circulate in and out of a cabinet, and that can be as good an idea in a kitchen as on a

boat. **Ted Timmer**, a builder/designer from Beacon, New York, says, "I was trying to play around with some design ideas as well as use materials that might be considered a bit more 'green' than the medium-density fiberboard (MDF) and veneer I usually see."

With that in mind, Ted made the cabinets of low-VOC bamboo plywood; for the face of this cabinet, he decided to go with a handwoven teak panel (see the top photo at left). (The teak was plantation-grown.) The project required ripping the teak into strips a heavy 1/16 in. thick; Ted played with a few different styles of weaves before settling on this one. After trimming the woven panels to fit, he set them into teak frames and applied the frame to the front of the pullout pantry.

Celebrating the grid

Joel Wheeler's shop in Albuquerque, New Mexico, built a kitchen designed by local architect Phil Custer. The majority of cabinets are faced with maple-frame doors and drawers divided by an irregular grid of 1/4-in. by 1/4-in. slots painted a deep green. Once the grid was laid out, Joel says the slots were cut on a tablesaw and cleaned up with an antique molding plane. The mitered frames were splined.

Custer says, "It was a small room, so part of the concept was that the lighter color creates a larger sense of space. To keep it from bleaching out, I added the geometrics." The glass cabinets (see the top photo on the facing page) were another strategy to break up the space. Glass stops applied to the exterior reinforced the grid concept and made the painting and glass installation easier.

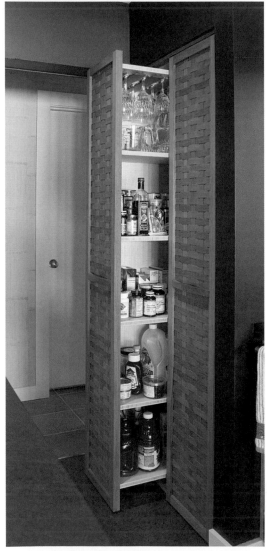

An arched teak handle (top) is tenoned into the stiles in place of a middle rail on this pull-out pantry cabinet.

A slightly different grid pattern on the glass doors fits with the pattern on the solid doors but makes the glass doors distinctive.

Deep green paint in the grooves grounds the light-colored cabinets.

Doorways can be special, too. The cabinet door rails make the entry to the garage fit in seamlessly.

Accentuate curves with more curves

To maximize space in a small kitchen, **Louis Mackall** of Breakfast Woodworks in Guilford, Connecticut, designed these cabinets around a doorway that leads to the garage. As Louis explains, "All entries are important, even those out back." The cabinets create an unusual detail that resembles a bulkhead leading down from the main deck of a boat. The lightly curved lower rails of the cabinet doors form an arch over the door. The thick partitions that form the stairway also have curves, this time a stronger design that crests like a wave at the top. Newel posts that resemble milk bottles anchor the partitions to the cabinets.

Installing Stock Cabinets

RICK GEDNEY

My father started working in the kitchen industry in the early 1950s. I spent many of my high-school days making cabinet deliveries and installing appliances. In 1979, he and I opened a small business together, Kitchens by Gedney. In one way or another, I've spent nearly 35 years designing, installing, and managing the installation of high-end kitchens.

A lot has changed in the kitchen industry since those early days. What hasn't changed is the demand for flawlessly installed cabinetry, a standard we've been committed to for nearly two generations.

Over the years, I—along with our skilled installation crews—have developed an approach to installing cabinets that ensures accuracy and quality. Here, I'll explain how to organize the job so that it keeps moving forward, how to prep the site properly, how to achieve an accurate layout, and how to install correctly the three most common types of kitchen cabinets: base cabinets, wall cabinets, and tall units that serve as pantries or that often house refrigerators or ovens.

Have a plan to stay organized

Whether in a remodel or a new home, the installation of kitchen cabinets involves high levels of stress and activity. In a remodel, you're occupying the space that makes the home habitable. Getting the job done as

quickly as possible is almost always the goal. In new construction, you're working amid a host of other subcontractors, all vying for space. In either environment, the room for error is significant. We keep our jobs accurate and in order with communication, a plan review, and a systems approach to installation.

Communication is critical. Create an installation calendar so that everyone involved in the project knows what's happening in the kitchen and when. Be sure to have established contacts with the cabinet supplier so that if a question or error arises, you can make a quick call to the person who can remedy the problem.

Before a single cabinet is uncrated, review the plan with your designer or cabinet supplier to be sure all cabinets are on site. Be sure you understand the supplier's terminology, because most cabinetmakers have their own codes and product numbers. Then be sure that all the labels actually match the cabinets in each package. Nobody wants to demolish a kitchen only to realize that the new corner base cabinet is the wrong size and that the correct unit is on back order for four weeks.

Establish a repetitive system, from site prep through installation, to be sure the job progresses as it should. Having a systematic approach makes cabinet installation more accurate, and it also saves time. With this system and two people on the job, expect to install the cabinetry for a typical kitchen in about three days. Another three days will likely be spent applying moldings, installing appliances, and completing ventilation work.

Protect finished surfaces

Install the cabinets when the kitchen is in a nearly finished state. The kitchen flooring should be installed before any cabinets are put in place. Wood floors should have one or two coats of finish on them. You can see the floor beneath many of today's professional-style appliances and furniturelike cabinets, so installing the floor first is smart. Also, the cabinets are finished, so it's foolish to try to maneuver a floor sander around the new units. The floor on this project is prefinished maple, so floor protection was critical. We've found success with products such as Ram Board® and Cover Guard®. Be sure all the seams are taped. Use painter's tape to secure the edges of each sheet to the floor.

TIP When connecting sheets of Ram Board, use Ram Board tape only. The adhesive is strong and nearly impossible to remove from tile, wood, and other finished materials.

Ideally, the ceiling in the kitchen should be primed and painted. The walls should be primed and have one finish coat, if possible. You'll have to do some touching up, but at least you won't risk paint splatter on the new cabinets and appliances while cutting in or painting large wall and ceiling areas.

Working in a fairly finished environment demands substantial care and dust control, especially during a remodel. Lose the tool belt to prevent scratches, and ensure all saws and sanders are connected to vacuums. A ZipWall® or other dust barrier should cordon off the kitchen. We place a dust collector outside the house and install a 12-in. flex duct in an open window. This creates negative pressure in the room and collects airborne dust. The unit is positioned far from the house, so everyone can talk or listen to music.

Work smart

In the old days, it was common practice to start a kitchen installation with the wall cabinets so that you didn't have to lean over the bases. In today's complex kitchens, we start with the base cabinets for several reasons.

Many kitchen designs call for wall cabinets to sit atop the counter. Establishing the height of the base cabinets is critical to getting boxes to fit properly. The height of most wall cabinets can be adjusted easily, while the height of bases and tall cabinets can't.

The base corner unit, if there is one, helps to establish the layout and determines how the upper and lower cabinets align. On this project, we started with the sink cabinet as our control. For the sink to line up perfectly with the middle stile of the window, the cabinet had to be dead center.

To expedite the project, countertop installers can come in as soon as the bases are put into place to make their templates. They can be working on the countertops while you're busy finishing the rest of the kitchen.

Finally, there isn't always an extra set of hands to help install the cabinets. Being able to prop a wall cabinet on a base unit to maneuver it into position is an easy, safe, and accurate way to work.

Step 1: Lay out the base cabinets

With plans in hand, draw the cabinetry layout on the wall. Layout lines not only serve as a template for the cabinet installation, but they also let you verify the plan. Be sure that vent, plumbing, and electrical locations are accurate. Mark stud locations during the layout phase to anticipate the need for extra blocking or additional cabinet support.

Find the high point in the floor, then mark the height of the base cabinets. Find the difference between the cabinet height and a laser-level line about 4 ft. above the floor. Use

Find the high point in the floor. Measure the distance between the floor and a laser-level line about 4 ft. above the floor to find the high and low points in the floor. The high point dictates the height of the base cabinets; use shims to compensate for the low points in the floor.

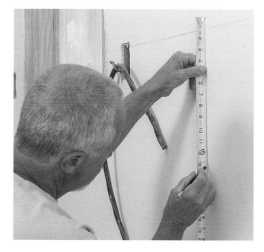

Mark the height of the bases. Measure the height of the cabinets, usually 34½ in., from the high point in the floor, and mark the wall. Measure the distance between the cabinet height and the laser line. Mark off the cabinet height around the room by measuring down off the laser-level line.

Draw a level line across the wall. Connect the marks on the wall with a level to establish a line to hold the base cabinets to during installation. This technique is more accurate than snapping chalklines or using a laser-level line.

Mark cabinet locations. Draw plumb lines on the wall to establish cabinet positions, taking care to be sure that cabinets such as the sink base align perfectly with the windows above.

the laser-level line to mark off the cabinet height around the room. This takes the uneven floor out of the equation. Use a level to connect the marks on the wall and mark the locations of the cabinets.

Step 2: Install the base cabinets

The first cabinet installed determines the placement of all the others. In most kitchens, it's important to start with a corner cabinet. If you save the corner cabinet for last and your layout is even the slightest bit off, it won't fit, and you'll be stuck waiting for a new, custom-built unit. Working away from a corner offers more flexibility. Instead of a cabinet, this kitchen has a sitting bench in the corner, so it offered some wiggle room. This project started with the next-most-critical cabinets in terms of layout: the sink

base and the cabinet beneath the range hood that holds the cooktop.

The first thing you need to do is measure the distance from the cabinet layout lines on

Modify for services. Transfer the vertical and horizontal measurements to the back or bottom of the cabinet.

Plumb and level the cabinet. With the cabinet in position, use a 4-ft. level to check if it's plumb (left). Place another level across the top of the cabinet to determine if it's level. Make adjustments with cedar shims (above). An applied toe kick scribed to the floor will hide any shims and gaps.

Fasten in place. The first cabinet is screwed to the wall (left), but all other cabinets are flushed to their adjacent units, screwed together with 1¼-in. #8 Twin Fast screws (right), and then screwed to the wall. Exposed fasteners are covered with Fastcaps.

the wall to the services coming through the wall or floor, then transfer the measurements to the cabinet. Cut a hole with a hole saw that's slightly larger than the size of the service line being accommodated.

Fit the cabinet to the wall. Once it's plumb and level, screw the cabinets in place. Screw cabinets to the wall through pilot holes in the hanging rail with 2½-in. #8 Twin Fast screws or a product with similar shear strength, but never with drywall screws.

Shims prevent the cabinet from being pulled out of alignment. On end cabinets where a toe kick is present, toenail a screw into the bottom plate.

Step 3: Scribe and secure tall cabinets

Pantry and tall cabinets that typically house ovens or refrigerators demand extra work to install correctly. Screwing the unit to studs would be enough, but sinking a few more screws into a plywood reinforcement strip offers insurance, especially when the cabinet is intended to house an oven that may have heavy doors.

The long side panels of these cabinets will expose every bump and dip in the wall if not scribed and cut to fit perfectly. Order these cabinets with end panels that are 3 in. to 4 in. wider than necessary to accommodate scribing. Having excess material offers a solid

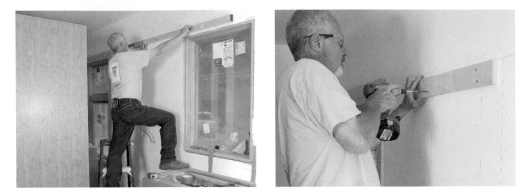

Strengthen the attachment to the wall. With the layout established on the wall, span studs with plywood reinforcement strips at the top of the unit. The cabinets will be screwed into them for extra support.

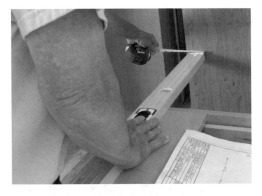

Calculate how much to trim. With the cabinet in place, use a level to represent the overhang of the counter on the adjacent base cabinet. The distance between the front edge of the level (photo at left) and the front edge of the cabinet determines how much material can be taken off the back of the cabinet's panels.

Scribe. With a compass and a sharp pencil, draw a continuous scribe line on each side panel of the cabinet.

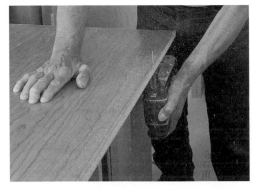

Cut the waste. Bulk material can be removed with a track-guided circular saw or a jigsaw (photo above). Follow the scribe line closely, but leave the pencil line.

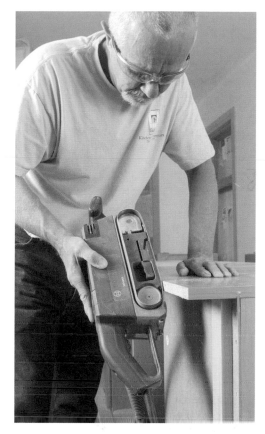

Use a box as a prop. With the cabinet's layout on the wall, position the cabinet atop a sturdy plywood box and plywood strips. Shim the box until it's level before setting a screw through the top and bottom hanging rails and into studs.

Bevel the edge. With a belt sander, remove the rest of the waste while giving the edge a bevel. Beveling the back of the panel ensures that the cabinet's outside edges will fit tight to the wall.

base for the saw to rest against when cutting to the scribe line, and it ensures plenty of play when fitting a cabinet against the most out-of-whack walls. These units typically stand proud of the other base cabinets so that countertops can die into their side panels.

Step 4: Hang wall cabinets safely

Some kitchen installers gang wall cabinets together on the ground and raise them in place with a lift or lots of helping hands. Installing wall cabinets one by one is also fine and is much more manageable when working alone or with one helper, but you will need a prop to help you hold the cabinet in place. Don't permanently secure the cabinet to the wall until you make sure it's plumb.

Check for plumb. Before completely securing the cabinet to the wall, make sure it's plumb so that the doors will work properly.

A Better Way to Build Wall Cabinets

GARRETT HACK

Imade this nice little wall-hung cabinet to hold tools, but it could easily find a spot inside a home and hold small knickknacks. What's interesting about this project is the uncommon way I build the case. The process is efficient, and it yields a

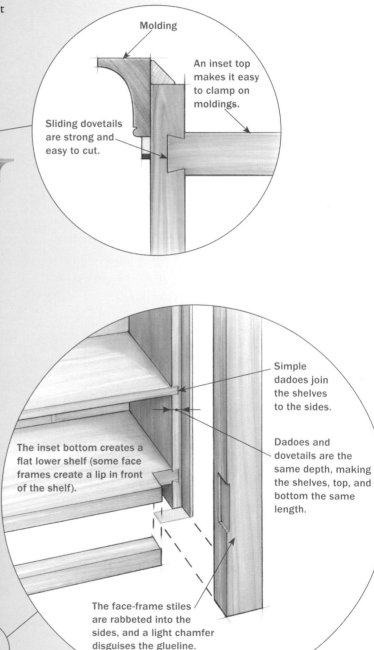

Molding

An inset top makes it easy to clamp on moldings.

Sliding dovetails are strong and easy to cut.

Simple dadoes join the shelves to the sides.

Dadoes and dovetails are the same depth, making the shelves, top, and bottom the same length.

The inset bottom creates a flat lower shelf (some face frames create a lip in front of the shelf).

The face-frame stiles are rabbeted into the sides, and a light chamfer disguises the glueline.

strong and very attractive piece with a lot of room for design variations.

The main joints are sliding dovetails, which are rock-solid and easily made with a tablesaw and router. Using sliding dovetails forces me to inset the top and bottom of the cabinet, but that works to my advantage, as you'll see.

Also, I use an unusual face-frame variation, which blends more seamlessly with the case. Basically, I cut a deep rabbet in the front edges of the case and glue the stiles into that rabbet. That leaves the glueline very close to the corner, where I can disguise it easily with a chamfer, a bead, or a bit of banding, for a variety of looks. Note that the rails are added later, simply glued to the top and bottom of the case. These also act as blocking for any moldings you want to add.

You might ask, why have a face frame at all? The first reason is that the sides are thin and a face frame allows you to create whatever thickness looks best at the front edges. Also, it lets you run through-dadoes for the shelves. Without a face frame, you would have to cut stopped dadoes to create a clean look at the front. Finally, it is easier to cut hinge mortises in the face-frame stiles while they are loose than it is to cut them in the sides themselves.

The design is best for hanging cabinets, but it works for floor-standing cabinets as well. The "ears" (the part of the sides that extends above the sliding dovetails) can be as short as ¾ in. and hidden behind a molding. Or an overhanging top can be added.

Banding determines the cabinet width

I often add a banding under the crown molding to serve as a transition between the molding and the case. It might seem like an unusual place to start, but to get the cabinet width and the length of the top and bottom

Size the case to the banding. To ensure that the banding ends with black stripes on each end, mill the banding stock first and tick off the exact case width on a story stick.

pieces, I need to know this banding length. The idea is to end up with a uniform black square on each end of the banding.

So after I ripped up the black and white pieces (ebony and holly) on the tablesaw, I laid out the sandwich and then used it to tick off the full banding length on a story stick (see the photo above). Then, to get the width

Elevation

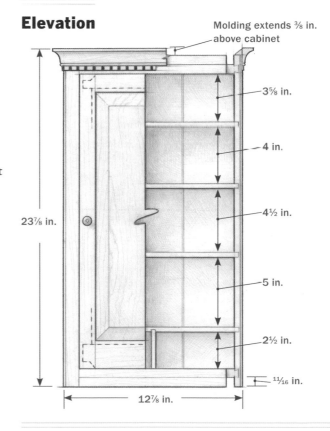

Molding extends ⅜ in. above cabinet

3⅝ in.

4 in.

4½ in.

5 in.

2½ in.

11⁄16 in.

23⅞ in.

12⅞ in.

Cabinet Construction

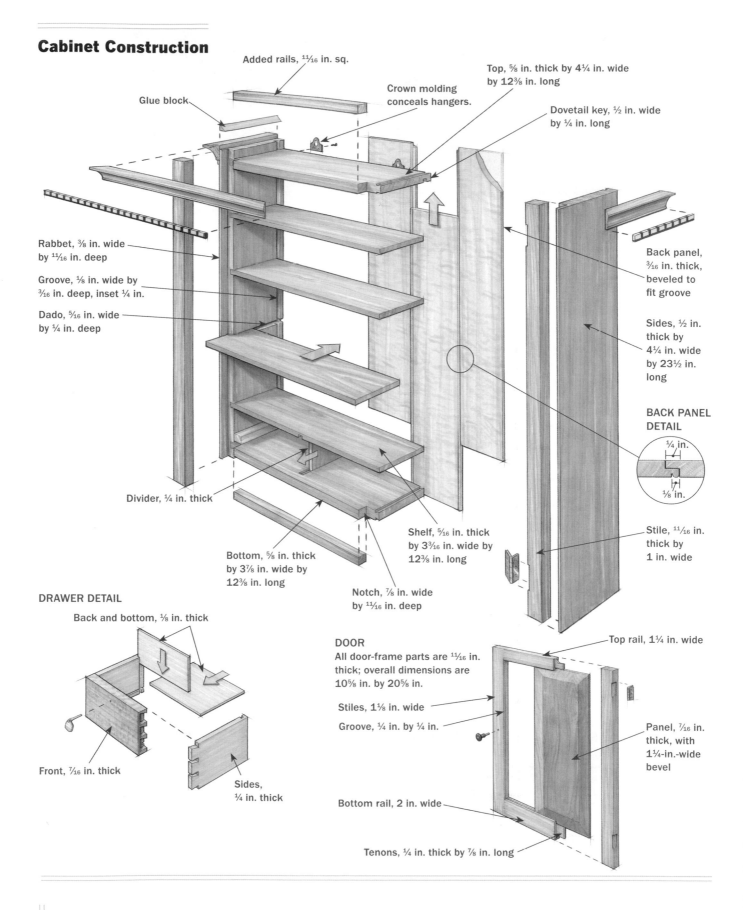

Added rails, $^{11}/_{16}$ in. sq.

Glue block

Crown molding conceals hangers.

Top, $^5/_8$ in. thick by $4^1/_4$ in. wide by $12^3/_8$ in. long

Dovetail key, $^1/_2$ in. wide by $^1/_4$ in. long

Rabbet, $^3/_8$ in. wide by $^{11}/_{16}$ in. deep

Groove, $^1/_8$ in. wide by $^3/_{16}$ in. deep, inset $^1/_4$ in.

Dado, $^5/_{16}$ in. wide by $^1/_4$ in. deep

Back panel, $^3/_{16}$ in. thick, beveled to fit groove

Sides, $^1/_2$ in. thick by $4^1/_4$ in. wide by $23^1/_2$ in. long

BACK PANEL DETAIL

$^1/_4$ in.

$^1/_8$ in.

Stile, $^{11}/_{16}$ in. thick by 1 in. wide

Divider, $^1/_4$ in. thick

Bottom, $^5/_8$ in. thick by $3^7/_8$ in. wide by $12^3/_8$ in. long

Notch, $^7/_8$ in. wide by $^{11}/_{16}$ in. deep

Shelf, $^5/_{16}$ in. thick by $3^3/_{16}$ in. wide by $12^3/_8$ in. long

DRAWER DETAIL

Back and bottom, $^1/_8$ in. thick

Front, $^7/_{16}$ in. thick

Sides, $^1/_4$ in. thick

DOOR
All door-frame parts are $^{11}/_{16}$ in. thick; overall dimensions are $10^5/_8$ in. by $20^5/_8$ in.

Stiles, $1^1/_8$ in. wide

Groove, $^1/_4$ in. by $^1/_4$ in.

Top rail, $1^1/_4$ in. wide

Panel, $^7/_{16}$ in. thick, with $1^1/_4$-in.-wide bevel

Bottom rail, 2 in. wide

Tenons, $^1/_4$ in. thick by $^7/_8$ in. long

Perfect alignment, guaranteed. To be sure all the dadoes and dovetail slots align perfectly, tape the sides together when you cut the joints (left). Start by cutting the sides to length on the tablesaw, then install a dado blade to cut the shelf dadoes (right). Cut the same 5/16-in.-wide dadoes at the sliding-dovetail locations. This will clear a path for the dovetail bit (below right).

of the cabinet, I had to subtract the slight overhang of the banding. Last, I marked the length of the crosspieces on the story stick. Because the dadoes and dovetails are the same depth, you can cut the shelves, top, and bottom to the same length with the same setup—another bonus.

Cut the joinery

Start with the sides of the case. Leave them a bit long and tape them together as shown in the photos above. Mark the finished length of the sides and lay out the dadoes for all the cross-pieces (even the sliding dovetails start out as dadoes). After cutting those dadoes, move to the router table to turn the dadoes for the top and bottom of the case into sliding dovetails. The next step is to cut the dovetail keys on the top and bottom of the case. Run both sides of the dovetail past the bit, and creep up on a nice fit. The dovetail key should slide partway in with only a small amount of pressure.

Now you can rabbet the sides and notch the top and bottom of the case for the face-frame stiles. Plane the stiles to fit perfectly later.

Rout the dovetail slots and keys. With the case sides still taped together, set a dovetail bit at the same height as the dadoes and rout the slots (top). Without moving the bit, adjust the fence to cut the keys in the case top and bottom (above).

A few more steps. After grooving the sides and top for the back panel, rabbet the sides for the face frame.

A raised back in three pieces

You can put any type of back into a cabinet like this, but I use a three-piece solid-wood back, shiplapped together. This lets me distribute the wood movement over four

gaps instead of two. It also allows me to add a bead to the joints that looks great inside the cabinet. I beveled the edges to fit into a small groove in the sides and top, making the back look like a raised panel.

Finish off the shelves

Now you can complete the shelves. They've been cut to final length, but should still be a little thick. Take time now to plane them by hand or power to fit their dadoes.

I add a vertical divider under the bottom shelf. That allows for two small drawers, or one drawer and an open shelf (see the drawing on p. 206). Note that the bottom dado for the divider doesn't extend all the way to the front, so it must be a stopped cut, made with a router.

Glue up in stages

Make sure all the parts are marked clearly so you know where they go and which end is which. Start with the shelves, then do the face frames. Move on to the divider and back. Use only a small amount of glue on the beginning of the dovetail slot and key. Too much will cause the joint to swell and bind. Check the case with a square as you assemble it.

Shelves first. Start by gluing the shelves into their dadoes and clamping them in place (left). Slide the case top and bottom into place from the rear (above).

Face frame comes next. Check the fit of the face-frame stiles, and then glue them into their rabbets (above left). Complete the face frame simply by gluing rails to the case top and bottom (above right).

Install the divider and back. Press the divider into place (above) and plane it flush after the glue has dried. The back consists of three shiplapped boards that are beveled to fit the grooves in the case sides and top. Slide them in from the bottom (right) and nail them to the shelves.

Finishing touches make the difference

There are lots of ways to finish off the top of a wall cabinet. It needs something; otherwise, it looks too much like a box. I used a cove molding, with that little banding just below it. One advantage of this case construction is the extra pieces (I call them "ears") that stick up beyond the sliding dovetail to give it

TIP It's easier to cut the mortises for the hinges in the stile before gluing it into the case.

How to make decorative banding

Glue up alternating strips of dark and light wood into a sandwich. Surface one side and crosscut the sandwich into ¼-in.-thick strips (1). Rip the crosscuts into ³⁄₁₆-in.-thick strips on the bandsaw (2). Clean up the saw marks with a block plane.

Starting at a corner, glue the banding in place one segment at a time (3). Rub a block of wood over the banding to seat it in place (4). No clamping is necessary. The author added a thin strip of ebony to the bottom edge of the banding to create a pleasing border. Again, simply rub it on to attach it (5).

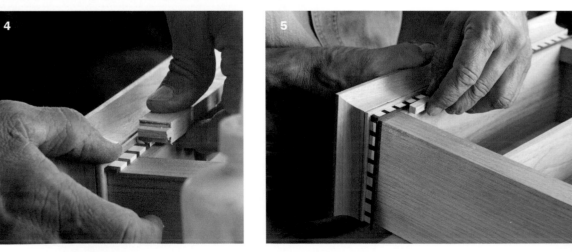

Add the molding. The "ears" that extend beyond the dovetailed case top provide a convenient clamping surface for the molding. A bead, cut with a scratch stock (above), is a nice transition for the banding.

Molding Detail

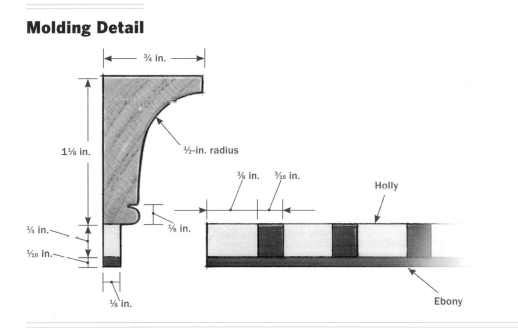

¾ in.

1⅛ in.

½-in. radius

⅜ in.   ³⁄₁₆ in.

Holly

¼ in.

⅛ in.

¹⁄₁₆ in.

Ebony

⅛ in.

strength. They are the perfect place to clamp those moldings. They were so short that I wasn't worried about cross-grain movement. With a deeper cabinet, I might screw them on from the inside, running the back screws through slotted holes. Of course, the front molding can always be glued on with no issues.

You can use any method you like for the door, drawer, and even the back of the cabinet. This approach to construction is very versatile, and works for cabinets of all sizes with all kinds of molding and decoration. That's why I love it.

A chamfer hides the glue joint. The author begins a stopped chamfer ½ in. below the molding. He starts the chamfer with a chisel, bevel down, and continues it to the bottom of the case with a block plane. Deepen the chamfer until one edge lines up with the glueline.

Another Corner Option

Cut a shallower rabbet in the case sides and fill the resulting space with a banding.

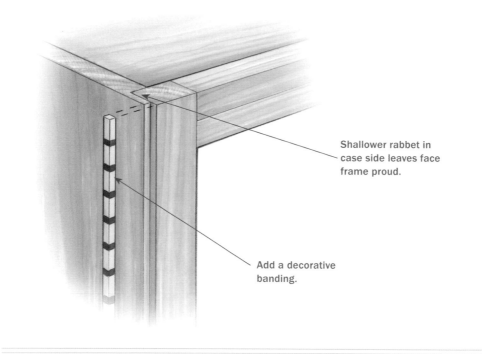

Shallower rabbet in case side leaves face frame proud.

Add a decorative banding.

Contributors

Rex Alexander is a cabinetmaker in Brethren, Michigan.

Christian Becksvoort is a contributing editor for *Fine Woodworking* magazine.

Brent Benner (www.roxburycabinet.com) is a cabinetmaker in Roxbury, Connecticut.

Charles Bickford is a senior editor at *Fine Homebuilding* magazine.

Anatole Burkin, former editor-in-chief of *Fine Woodworking*, is the vice president of digital content for The Taunton Press.

Steve Casey (www.stevecaseydesign.com) designs and builds cabinetry in Los Angeles County.

Rick Gedney owns Kitchens by Gedney (www.gedneykitchens.com) in Madison, Connecticut.

Scott Gibson works mostly in his shop, a short walk from his house in East Waterboro, Maine.

Garrett Hack is a contributing editor for *Fine Woodworking* magazine.

Sven Hanson is a cabinetmaker in Marietta, Georgia, and Albuquerque, New Mexico.

Nancy R. Hiller runs a custom-cabinet shop in Bloomington, Indiana (www.nrhillerdesign.com).

Anissa Kapsales is a former associate editor at *Fine Woodworking*.

Joseph Lanza is an architect, builder, and cabinetmaker. He lives in Duxbury, Massachusetts.

Steve Latta teaches furniture making at Thaddeus Stevens College in Lancaster, Pennsylvania.

Mike Maines is a designer in Yarmouth, Maine.

Martin Milkovits is a furniture maker in Mason, New Hampshire.

Tony O'Malley, a woodworker in Emmaus, Pennsylvania, specializes in making custom built-ins.

Gregory Paolini makes Arts and Crafts furniture in Waynesville, North Carolina.

Andy Rae is a woodworker and author of *The Complete Illustrated Guide to Furniture & Cabinet Construction* (The Taunton Press 2004) and *Building Doors and Drawers* (The Taunton Press, 2007).

Gary Striegler is a builder in Fayetteville, Arkansas.

Matthew Teague is a professional furniture maker and writer in Nashville, Tennessee.

Credits

All photos are courtesy of *Fine Homebuilding* magazine (FHB), © The Taunton Press, Inc., or *Fine Woodworking* (FWW) magazine, © The Taunton Press, Inc., except as noted below:

Front cover: photo by Scott Gibson (FHB). Back cover: photo by Thomas McKenna (FWW). Drawing by John Hartman (FWW).

The articles in this book appeared in the following issues of *Fine Homebuilding* and *Fine Woodworking*:

pp: 4-8: Build Better Cabinets with the Best Plywood by Matthew Teague, FHB issue 210. Photos by Rodney Diaz (FHB), except pgs. 7 (bottom) and 9 courtesy of Columbia Forest Products. Drawing by Bill Godfrey (FHB).

pp: 9-16: Illustrated Guide to Drawers by Matthew Teague, FWW issue 201. Photos and drawings by John Tetreault (FWW).

pp. 17-23: Illustrated Guide to Doors by Andy Rae, FWW issue 204. Photo by Michael Pekovich (FWW). Drawings by Christopher Mills (FWW).

pp. 24-32: Hang It Up by Anissa Kapsales, FWW issue 201. Photos by FWW staff, except pgs. 28 (bottom) and 29 (top left, top center) by Dennis Griggs (FWW). Drawings by John Hartman (FWW).

pp. 33-42: Do an About-Face on Cabinets by Steve Latta, FWW issue 217. Photos by Steve Scott (FWW). Drawings by Bob La Pointe (FWW).

pp. 43-52: A Portable Book Rack by Greg Paolini, FWW issue 197. Photos by David Heim (FWW), except p. 43 by John Tetreault (FWW). Drawings by Christopher Mills (FWW).

pp. 53-61: Quick, Sturdy Bookcase by Martin Milovits, FWW issue 194. Photos by Thomas McKenna (FWW). Drawings by John Hartman (FWW).

pp. 62-69: Bookcases Transform an Unused Wall by Brent Benner, FHB issue 222. Photos by Charles Bickford (FHB), except pp. 68-69 by Rob Yagid (FHB). Drawing p. 63 by Brent Benner (FHB).

pp. 70-81: Sleek Console Built for Today's TVs by Anatole Burkin, FWW issue 214. Photos by Thomas McKenna (FWW), except pgs. 71 and 79 (bottom right) by Michael Pekovich (FWW). Drawings by Bob La Pointe (FWW).

pp. 82-91: A Low Console for a Home Theater by Steve Casey, FWW issue 200. Photos by Steve Scott (FWW), except pgs. 83, 84 (top right, bottom left) by Dean Della Ventura (FWW). Drawings by John Hartman (FWW).

pp. 92-97: Straight-Ahead Corner Hutch by Gary Striegler, FHB issue 184. Photos by Brian Pontolilo (FHB), except p. 92 by Rick Green (FHB). Drawings by Bob La Pointe (FHB).

pp. 98-108: Beautify Your Home with a Shaker Built-In by Christian Becksvoort, FWW issue 221. Photos by Anissa Kapsales (FWW), except p. 98 by Michael Pekovich (FWW). Drawings by Bob La Pointe (FWW).

pp. 109-120: Mudroom Built-In by Tony O'Malley, FWW issue 213. Photos by Thomas McKenna (FWW). Drawings by Bob La Pointe (FWW).

pp. 121-130: A Clever Kitchen Built-In by Nancy R. Hiller, FHB issue 193. Photos by Kendall Reeves (FHB). Drawings by Bob La Pointe (FWW).

pp. 131-137: Built-Ins, Anywhere by Gary Striegler, FHB issue 212. Photos by Charles Bickford (FHB). Drawing by John Hartman (FHB).

pp. 138-141: Maximize Pantry Storage by Rex Alexander, FHB issue 185. Photo by Dietrich Floeter (FHB). Drawings by Bob La Pointe (FHB).

pp. 142-148: Taming an Outdated Pantry by Joseph Lanza, FHB issue 217. Photos by Charles Bickford (FHB). Drawings by John Hartman (FHB).

pp. 149-155: Add Storage to Your Stair Rail by Scott Gibson, FHB issue 213. Photos by Scott Gibson (FHB). Drawings by John Hartman (FHB).

pp. 156-164: Six Rules for Fast and Foolproof Cabinetmaking by Sven Hanson, FHB issue 177. Photos by Daniel S. Morrison (FHB), except pp. 156-157 by Robert Reck (FHB)

pp. 165-173: A Faster Easier Approach to Custom Cabinets by Mike Maines, FHB issue 200. Photos by Rob Yagid (FHB). Drawing by Bob La Pointe (FHB).

pp. 174-179: Four Quick Cabinet Upgrades by Gary Striegler, FHB issue 214. Photos by Chris Ermides (FHB), except pp. 174-175 by Bryan Striegler (FHB).

pp. 180-187: Cabinet Door Shoot-Out by Scott Gibson and Joseph Lanza, FHB issue 220. Photos by Charles Bickford (FHB), except p. 180 and p. 181 (inset photos) by Rodney Diaz (FHB).

pp. 188-196: Signature Details for Kitchen Cabinets by Charles Bickford, FHB issue 189. Photos by Charles Bickford (FHB), except p. 194 by Chris Ermides (FHB). Drawings by Dan Thornton (FHB).

pp. 197-203: Installing Stock Cabinets by Rick Gedney, FHB issue 223. Photos by Rob Yagid (FHB).

pp. 204-212: A Better Way to Build Cabinets by Garrett Hack, FWW issue 210. Photos by Michael Pekovich (FWW). Drawings by Bob La Pointe (FWW).

Index

Note: Page numbers in *italics* indicate projects.

If you like this book, you'll love *Fine Woodworking*.